THE ELEMENTS OF PLAYWRITING

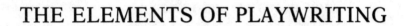

OTHER BOOKS BY LOUIS E. CATRON

THE
ELEMENTS
OF
PLAYWRITING

Louis E. Catron

Macmillan Publishing Company
New York

Maxwell Macmillan Canada
Toronto

Maxwell Macmillan International
New York   Oxford   Singapore   Sydney

To my mother

Macmillan Publishing Company   Maxwell Macmillan Canada, Inc.
866 Third Avenue   1200 Eglinton Avenue East, Suite 200
New York, NY 10022   Don Mills, Ontario M3C 3N1

Macmillan Publishing Company is part of the Maxwell Communication Group of Companies.

Library of Congress Cataloging-in-Publication Data
Catron, Louis E.
    The elements of playwriting / Louis E. Catron.
        p.   cm.
    Includes index.
    ISBN 0-02-522991-5
    1. Playwriting.   I. Title.
PN1661.C367   1993
808.2—dc20   92-31037
                                        CIP

Macmillan books are available at special discounts for bulk purchases for sales promotions, premiums, fund-raising, or educational use. For details, contact:
                Special Sales Director
                Macmillan Publishing Company
                866 Third Avenue
                New York, NY 10022

10   9   8   7   6   5   4   3   2   1
Printed in the United States of America

Writers at Work
(Part One)

STAN: *My head is tightening up. I'm all constricted inside. I just can't think.* (He thinks, then looks at EUGENE.) *This is hard, Gene. Really hard.*
EUGENE: I *know.*
STAN: I *won't give up if you don't give up.*
EUGENE: I *won't give up.*
STAN: I *love being a writer.*
EUGENE: Me, *too.*
STAN: *It's just the writing that's hard. . . . You know what I mean?*
EUGENE: Yeah.

NEIL SIMON
Broadway Bound

Contents

Acknowledgments   xi

Introduction   xiii

1. Being a Playwright   1

Being a Playwright Means Appreciating Your Ancestry • Being a Playwright Starts with a Personal Statement of "This I Believe" • Being a Playwright Means Identifying Human Traits You Admire or Dislike • Being a Playwright Involves a Sense of Construction • Being a Playwright Means Writing Stageworthy Plays, Not "Closet Dramas" • Being a Playwright Requires Understanding—Although Not Always Following—Rules and Guidelines • Theatrical Directors Describe What They Look For in Plays • Being a Playwright Means Writing, Writing, and Writing • Playwrights Describe Their Work Habits • Special Advantages of Being a Playwright • Exercises

2. What Makes a Play?   17

Definition of a Play • A Play Is Not a Novel • Plays Require Conflict • Selectivity: Drama Is an Interpretation of Life, Not Real Life • Plays Are Complete in Themselves • Plays Have a Beginning, Middle, and End • Avoid Cinematic Writing • Dramatic Action Must Be Possible, Plausible, and Probable • Plays Are Entertainment • Plays Communicate with Emotions • Plays Communicate to the Imagination • Unities of Time, Place, and Action • The Fourth (and Most Important) Unity: Playwright's Purpose • Exercises

3. The Size of Your Canvas: Monodramas, One-Acts, and Full-Length Plays

36

Determining the Size of Your Canvas • The Monodrama • The One-Act Play • The Full-Length Play • Thinking of Audiences and Types of Theatres for Your Play • Exercises

4. Where Do You Start? Turning Your Ideas into Plays

49

Sources of Ideas: Situation, Character, or Theme • Working with Your Germinal Ideas • Fleshing Out Germinal Ideas • The "Magic If" Stimulates Creativity • Do Your Ideas Have Theatrical Potential? • Exercises

5. Creating Characters: People in Action to Achieve Their Goals

64

Writing Characters to Attract Producers, Directors, and Actors • The Playwright as Actor: Using the Actor's Approaches to Characterization • Sources for Theatrical Characters • Necessary Characters for Your Play • The Protagonist • The Antagonist • Secondary Characters Serve the Play • Creating Theatrical Characters • Deciding How Many Characters You Need in Your Play • Exercises

6. Building Plot: Shaping Your Play's Action   94

Three Basic Divisions of Plot • Part One: Beginning—Introductory Materials • Part Two: Middle—The Play's Struggles and Action • Part Three: Ending—A Sense of Finality • Exercises Using Other Plays • Exercises for the Play You Are Writing

7. Constructing Dialogue: Action Through Words

122

What Is Dialogue? • Theatrical Dialogue Differs from Other Forms of Writing • The Playwright's Goals • Acquiring an Ear for Dialogue • Communicating Basic Details • Techniques of Writing Dialogue • Principles of Structural Emphasis • Special Aspects of Dialogue: Imagery and Poetry, Monologues and Soliloquies • Dangers to Avoid • Working with Actors and Directors • Exercises

8. Evaluating and Revising Your Play   153

The Revision Process for All Writers • Working Alone to Revise Your Play • Working with Others to Revise Your Play • A Checklist of Questions to Consider at Each Step of Revision • The Play's Overall Effect • Characterization • Dialogue • Plot • The Play's Beginning, Middle, and End • Desired Audience Response

9. Script Format: Typing Your Script for Producers and Directors   170

General Guidelines • Specific Guidelines for the Playscript • Preliminary Pages • The Script Itself • Sample Pages from a Script • Mailing Your Play

10. Resources for the Playwright   186

Organizations for Playwrights • Copyright • Literary Agents • Sources to Help You Find Producers, Publishers, Agents, Contests, and Workshops • Periodicals • Contests, Workshops, Seminars, and Conferences • Productions • Income • Publication • Conclusion

Index   213

Acknowledgments

Special thanks are due to Michael Sullivan, a good friend and a literate gentleman, for his suggestions and encouragement that started this book.

I am indebted to those who reviewed the manuscript and made excellent critical suggestions. Although any errors remain mine, this book's contents reflect their expert insights into the art, craft, and business of playwriting.

In particular I appreciate the generous suggestions and comments from William Talbot, senior editor at Samuel French, Inc.; Robert A. Freedman of the Robert A. Freedman Dramatic Agency, Inc., and an officer of the Association of Authors' Representatives; Gillian Richards, literary coordinator for the Theatre Communications Group; Dana S. Singer, director of business affairs for the Dramatists Guild, Inc.; Mollie Ann Meserve, president of Feedback Theatrebooks; and Steve Soderberg, head, Information Office, and other information specialists in the Copyright Office at the Library of Congress.

Richard Palmer, my colleague at the College of William and Mary, was constantly available to read chapters in progress, make insightful recommendations, and discuss the art and mysteries of theatre.

Beth C. Mills, at the office of the William and Mary Department of Theatre and Speech, deserves special thanks for her patient and thorough proofreading of the manuscript.

Natalie Chapman, senior editor at Macmillan, was especially helpful with her thoughtful questions and recommendations, always directly on target, always supportive and encouraging.

Finally, I am most grateful to the William and Mary students with whom I've worked in classes and theatrical productions. Over the years their probing questions, earnest discussions, and eagerness to create good theatre have continually educated me.

Introduction

*I regard the theatre as the greatest of all art forms, the most
immediate way in which a human being can share with another
the sense of what it is to be a human being. The supremacy of
the theatre derives from the fact that it is always "now" on the
stage.*

THORNTON WILDER

A creative writer is a spelunker of ideas who enjoys poking
through uncharted caves, using the bright light of curiosity
to illuminate unfamiliar caverns and bypasses, following twisting thoughts simply to discover where they lead. Your expedi-
tion may uncover brilliant new treasures, sparkling gems that
create a powerful story with fascinating characters. Or it may
end at cul-de-sacs that go nowhere, making you grope back to
the beginning to start again, yet wiser and enriched for the
search.

Is there a map that guarantees you'll discover the right passage
to writing your play?

No.

Despite fervent and even dictatorial advice you'll often find in
playwriting books or hear from other writers, no single exploratory
system works for all writers all the time. There are certain guidelines that can help you, however, and *The Elements of Playwriting*
shows you specific approaches that will help you bring your play
to life while avoiding dead-end paths.

Whether you're a beginning writer starting your first exploration into playwriting or a more experienced playwright seek-

ing new insight into improving plays you've completed, you'll find that *The Elements of Playwriting* gives you practical guidelines, insightful quotations from writers and directors, numerous examples from classical and modern plays, and exercises that will help you be a playwright. Direct references to what producers, directors, and actors look for in plays will help you write for specific theatrical needs, aiding you to become a *produced* playwright.

This book explores what being a playwright means—expressing your personal point of view, bringing your vision to life, developing dimensional characters, structuring your play's action, creating effective dialogue, and finding producers, directors, and actors to bring your work to life. The book's goal is to help you create powerful theatrical excitement through writing monodramas, one-acts, and full-length plays.

Being a playwright means understanding that writing is the route to learning—about playwriting, of course, but also about yourself and your world. Being a playwright means writing, searching for your ideas. *Writing leads to writing.* Never feel discouraged if your play doesn't jump full-blown into existence. Plays seldom do. If you don't have a precise grasp of what to write, write to discover what you want to write.

This book contains numerous exercises to help you make those discoveries about yourself as well as about the art of writing plays. The exercises guide you through the writing process so you can, as playwright Thornton Wilder says, use theatre to share with another what it is to be a human being. Do the exercises carefully, please, because they are constructed with progressive steps to lead you through the maze of playwriting.

Be patient with your progress. Years of training and study are necessary to become a brain surgeon or a lawyer. Playwriting is no less challenging or demanding, and you should expect to learn your craft through constant writing, experimentation, and study.

This book will help you learn the playwright's art and craft, appreciate the similarities and differences between playwriting and other forms of creative writing, respect the work of your theatrical colleagues who give of themselves to bring your play to life, and (in keeping with Thornton Wilder's quotation that begins this preface) honor the theatre as humanity's most significant art.

You'll also find answers to questions playwrights frequently ask, tips about writing techniques, and suggestions to help you avoid pitfalls.

The Elements of Playwriting is based on the premise that anyone, regardless of age or education, can learn techniques of playwriting, providing you bring convictions about your world, motivation and perseverance, a love of theatre, a deep desire to learn and improve while remaining patient with your learning process, and a driving hunger to express your ideas in theatrical form. You also must want to learn playwriting's basic rules and guidelines that help you become a master storyteller.

Paradoxically, playwriting is a creative art that defies rules, yet it is an exacting craft that must follow theatre's basic (and, all things considered, valuable) restrictions. Any text on playwriting must choose between a prescriptive approach that states "here's the only way to write your play" and a freewheeling approach that tells the writer to "just do your own thing" but gives little or no concrete help. This book suggests a sensible compromise between the extremes of rigidity and freewheeling.

Start by learning the rules and guidelines. Understand why they exist. Accept the fact that they help you create stageworthy plays. Then feel free to violate them according to the demands of your play and the theatre's requirements, but not simply to follow fads or to be different for the sake of difference.

It is certainly easier to tell you that there are no principles, no rules, no guidelines, no discipline in the art and craft of playwriting. Some theorists tell you that modern writing is freewheeling, that the concept of "action" is out of date, and that the works of some modern writers prove that great plays can be written without dramatic tension, conflict, or action.

Those opinions are—let's be blunt—products of muddled, wrongheaded thinking. One suspects that such theorists have never gotten into actually writing or staging plays (or if they did, they did it poorly). Perhaps they look at plays as if they are "literature." But plays are not literature, except in secondary ways. Plays are written for the stage, and one test of any script is simple: Is it stageworthy? The various rules, guidelines, and disciplines exist for one reason: to help playwrights construct stageworthy plays.

I bring to this book years of experience as a theatrical director and playwriting and acting teacher. I've directed over 150 plays and musicals and supervised productions of perhaps half again that number, including original plays, and I've written books on playwriting and play direction as well as articles in national writers' magazines. That experience teaches me that playwriting, acting, and directing, often viewed as separate disciplines, share so many similarities that knowledge of one feeds knowledge of the others. These pages reflect those years of stage experience.

Being a playwright means, after all, writing *stageworthy* plays. You must know what actors and directors look for in a play, as well as what makes them reject a script. You write in theatrical form so those theatre artists can transform your play from the page to the stage for an audience.

Writing stageworthy plays is a challenging goal in itself, but it is more difficult because of the influences of television and motion pictures. According to various estimates, the average person has viewed more than nineteen thousand hours of television by the time he or she graduates from high school. Add thousands more hours watching movies. As a result, cinematic writing techniques are implanted in that person's subconscious. It's a powerful form of brainwashing that the playwright must combat. You must want to write for the stage, not TV, although learning playwriting is an excellent approach to screenwriting.

Theatrical agents, producers, directors, play publishers, and contest judges report they are distressed to receive an ever-increasing number of nonstageworthy scripts that ignore the theatre's special strengths and instead are based on cinematic writing techniques. Characteristics of TV-influenced playscripts include narrow and stereotyped characters, incomplete action and fragmentary scenes written to fit around commercial breaks, blandly noncontroversial topics to avoid offending advertisers, rapid and repeated shifts in time and place that film easily achieves but theatre does not, scenes that do not end but seem to need the music that accompanies a TV close-up of a character's face as the screen fades to a blackout, "opening up" the script to encompass panoramic concepts in contrast to theatre's focus on detail, not very funny one-liners that require an artificial laugh-track, and even camera movements and zoom lens effects.

This book stresses avoiding cinematic writing by writing *stage-*

worthy plays. We define the term from several points of view. We stress theatrical needs. We indicate rules and guidelines that help you write for live theatre. Most important, we continually illustrate points with references to the directors and actors who will bring your play to life on stage.

Certain premises underlie this book. We can state them briefly here as a guide to the following chapters.

- Anyone can learn to write a play. Playwriting offers equal opportunity employment, open to all, and blind to sex, race, religion, national origin, occupation, educational background, and age.
- Drama is the art of the showdown. Conflict, in one form or another, is an essential quality for effective playwriting.
- The playwright is first and foremost a storyteller. He or she may be a philosopher, theologian, psychologist, historian, biographer; the playwright may seek to evoke political or social change; or the playwright may want to amuse or anger audiences. Always, though, the playwright is a master storyteller in the tradition of the ancient shaman, using theatrical magic to captivate audiences while illuminating certain mysteries of their world.
- Although books on writing often recommend that you should "write about what you know best," better advice is to "write about what you believe." Selecting subjects and characters that are highly important to you will make playwriting easier and more enjoyable. Writing a personal passion will give your play more fire and significance, making it more appealing to producers and audiences.
- Bad writing isn't protected by calling it experimental. Learn why playwriting's rules have evolved before venturing into new forms.
- Although playwrights may have heard "show, don't tell," a number of times, the advice deserves emphasis through repetition.
- Avoid the "Broadway mentality." Literally thousands of professional and amateur theatres exist across the country, and your

goal should be *production*, not necessarily Broadway production.

Most important, although playwriting is difficult, you'll find that creating your own world peopled with characters you invent, who are involved in conflict and actions you share, is, simply, *fun*.

Hard work? Certainly.

Frustrating? Often.

Challenging? Very.

But fun nonetheless, even addictive.

Enjoy writing. The act itself is deeply rewarding, and you'll feel remarkably satisfied each time you complete a good scene or develop a rich character or finish your play.

Your rewards go further. Seeing your play come to life onstage is a remarkable experience that you will treasure the rest of your life.

You'll find, I hope, that *The Elements of Playwriting* is a helpful book that marries concepts with practical, concrete suggestions, showing you how to write plays that will bring you that exciting experience.

> *Looking back, I imagine I was always writing. Twaddle it was, too. But better far write twaddle or anything, anything, than nothing at all.*
>
> —Katherine Mansfield

> *I wanted to get to learn the technique of the theatre so well that I could then forget about it. I always feel it's not wise to violate rules until you know how to observe them.*
>
> —T. S. Eliot

THE ELEMENTS OF PLAYWRITING

1

Being a Playwright

I see the playwright as a lay preacher peddling the ideas of his time in popular form.

AUGUST STRINDBERG

Never fear [the audience] nor despise it. Coax it, charm it, interest it, stimulate it, shock it now and then if you must, make it laugh, make it cry, but above all ... never, never, never bore the living hell out of it.

NOËL COWARD

How do you become a playwright? What makes a "good" play? Where do you start? How does writing plays differ from writing essays, novels, or short stories? What techniques do professional writers recommend? What do you look for to revise your play? What do producers and directors look for in your play?

This book answers these and comparable questions. Here we examine what it means to "be a playwright." Later chapters discuss other aspects of the playwright's art and craft, constructing your play to suit theatre's special needs, shaping your ideas into theatrical form, bringing characters to life, and writing effective dialogue.

BEING A PLAYWRIGHT MEANS APPRECIATING YOUR ANCESTRY

When you become a playwright you join an elite group of civilization's most accomplished artists. Your oldest ancestor is the prehistoric shaman who used magic, costume, and pantomime-dance to enact scenes that enlightened tribal members trying to understand the mysteries of a confusing and sometimes hostile universe. Like that witch doctor of the past, you are a master storyteller who uses a special form of theatrical magic to communicate to audiences, giving them insight into a world that is no less confusing for being modern, and illuminating mysteries that surround us.

You enter an arena made famous by playwrights who have been revered for their insightful, powerful tales of humans struggling not merely to survive but to endure. You join Sophocles, Aristophanes, Molière, William Shakespeare, Henrik Ibsen, George Bernard Shaw, Lillian Hellman, Tennessee Williams, Arthur Miller, Neil Simon, and thousands of others whose plays shape public opinion, awake emotions, stimulate thought, and enlighten, amuse, and captivate millions.

You write for a unique art that over centuries has made major contributions to human growth and enjoyment. The theatre's accomplishments are remarkable, as Frank Whiting says in *An Introduction to the Theatre*:

> Without quibbling over which is the greatest of the arts, let us remember that the theatre makes its appeal on two levels: the aesthetic and the intellectual. On the aesthetic level the theatre, like music, painting, and dancing, makes its contribution to the emotional needs of man and to his hunger for the beautiful. On the intellectual level a tremendous proportion of the greatest ideas ever expressed by man have been expressed in dramatic form. Students of philosophy study Aeschylus, Goethe, Ibsen, and Shaw, as well as Plato, Schopenhauer, Nietzsche, and Dewey. No other branch of human learning can point with pride to a more impressive list of great names. No other field of literature can quite equal the drama in the total extent of its contributions.

Whiting's description of theatre's contributions is focused on playwrights, leaders in theatre's growth. Although his list of great playwrights is impressive, we can add more. For example, students of psychology study Sophocles and Shakespeare and use plays such as *Electra* and *Oedipus* to identify psychological dysfunctions such as the "Electra" and "Oedipal" complexes. Equally significant lists can be cited for theology, history, politics, sociology, biography, and other fields. Throughout history playwrights have been active in social protest and movements for reform in politics, society, medicine, economics, and the like.

One way to become aware of your ancestors' many contributions is to read their plays, selecting playwrights who have written about topics and characters that intrigue you. Reading alone is not enough, however, and you should see plays in production, carefully observing the writing techniques that make them come to life from page to stage.

BEING A PLAYWRIGHT STARTS WITH A PERSONAL STATEMENT OF "THIS I BELIEVE"

Membership in the distinguished community of playwrights starts with developing keen insight into your personal beliefs, attitudes, and standards. These provide the subjects and themes of your plays. You also examine your beliefs about human behavior, deciding what you think are admirable or disreputable traits. These concepts lead you to create characters you'll believe in and care about. Those two steps give your plays special meaning and make them original works.

Being a playwright begins with a strong need to communicate your deepest personal beliefs. A play that boils up from your inner self will be stronger because it expresses ideas important to you; and the writing process will be easier and more enjoyable because you'll *want* to write, which will help motivate you to establish daily writing goals and maintain a writer's self-discipline. You want your plays to appeal to others—writing for the theatre is based on a desire to communicate—but that doesn't imply you diminish your own values by writing to please others. You first satisfy your own drive to communicate what you believe is important.

Theatrical excitement is a product of the playwright's passion and commitment. Think of your play as a personalized statement of your inner core, who you are, what you believe, your vision of the world around you. Write plays dealing with ideas and people that are most important to you. Substance comes with "I have an idea I *must* express through the stage," not "I'll write a play." The latter is an exercise; the former, a passion. Exercises are valuable learning tools to help you develop technique, but your goal is larger: You want to use the theatre to show your particular vision of your world. Personal involvement with your play's subject will be contagious, attracting producers, directors, actors, and audiences who will share your interest.

Identify Your Beliefs

Before you begin writing, identify what is most important to you, a process that for many playwrights is an insightful journey into self-discovery. Spend as much time as necessary writing your personal credo, a statement of your deepest convictions, beliefs, and standards. Although preparing your statement of "This I Believe" may take several weeks and result in dozens of pages, the investment of time and effort will net a rich return when you write your plays. Your credo becomes a treasure chest of precious jewels and gold that you use to create glittering characters and rich situations for effective plays.

Your written statement of convictions is deeply personal—there are no right or wrong beliefs—and focuses on topics that are highly important to you. For example, your credo may deal with such matters as family, love, or marriage; an individual's ambition, goals, and future; the significance of past experiences, loves, or hates; what it means to be selfish or giving; social problems such as AIDS, unwanted pregnancy and abortion, drugs, or the homeless; ethical dilemmas between right and wrong; and aspects of religion, relationship with a deity, or attitudes about false prophets.

Organize Your Beliefs by Priorities

When you've completed the first step of identifying your beliefs, it is time to put them in an order or priority, deciding which are most important to you. Make those the subjects of the plays you'll write. Only after you've identified your ideas can you think of playwriting's rules, techniques, conventions, and standards, or producers, directors, and agents. Start your journey into being a playwright with a need to express a passion, and write about a fire that ignites your inner being. (For more detail about writing your beliefs, you are invited to read "The Credo," chapter 4 of my book, *Playwriting*, Prospect Heights, Illinois: Waveland Press, 1990.)

BEING A PLAYWRIGHT MEANS IDENTIFYING HUMAN TRAITS YOU ADMIRE OR DISLIKE

Personal convictions, although highly important, are not enough for the playwright. Convictions, after all, can lead to essays, which *tell* the reader a point of view. You want to write plays that *show* those significant aspects of life. Being a playwright requires you to translate your abstract convictions into concrete, dimensional, interesting characters who demonstrate those beliefs through theatrical conflict, using actions and inactions, speeches and silences. Effective playwriting is based on the writer's fascination with human psychology, looking closely at people around you (including yourself, family, and friends) and the fictional characters who live in your imagination, awaiting your invitation to come to life in your plays.

Just as one major factor in becoming a playwright is identifying issues important to you, so an equally important part is recognizing the specific *human traits* you believe are most significant— characteristics you admire, respect, and love, as well as the qualities you dislike, reject, or despise. Awareness of these traits leads you to create dimensional characters in your play, and your beliefs about people help you create characters with qualities that are important to you, making you want, even need, to write.

Think about plays you have read or productions you have seen, and you'll find that you're remembering the characters. The Macbeths, Hamlets, Laura Wingfields, and Willy Lomans remain in audiences' memories because the playwrights' attitudes and beliefs about people created moving, interesting, memorable characters who often seem to have a real-life existence beyond the confines of the stage. Perhaps you'll want to use playwriting to create characters who fulfill your expectations, as Ayn Rand did; she said she wrote *The Fountainhead* and *Atlas Shrugged* to create people she could admire.

Identify Human Traits You Admire and Dislike

What do you believe are the most admirable qualities in humans? What qualities do you strongly dislike? Write lists of those personality attributes. For example, one playwright's list of positive traits could include generosity, bravery, and kindness, with negative qualities such as cowardice, lying, and cruelty. Your lists may be quite different. Take your time constructing lists of these qualities. This investigatory process deserves your unhurried attention because you are investing your personal standards in your play, giving your characters your own special voice.

Actions Show Traits

When you've completed your list of positive and negative traits, add the actions that show each trait. For example, "generosity" is merely a label, a loose term that doesn't specify character. Define it by acts: What does the character actually do that shows generosity? In what circumstances is he or she generous? What educational or environmental factors motivate the character to be generous? One good way to define traits with theatrical action is to assume a stranger is observing your character: What would he or she do to make that stranger conclude the character is generous?

Continue illustrating each positive and negative trait by actions until you've completed your lists. Some of the qualities will become significant aspects of characters in plays you'll write.

The man who writes about himself and his own time is the only man who writes about all people and about all time.
—George Bernard Shaw

BEING A PLAYWRIGHT INVOLVES A SENSE OF CONSTRUCTION

Writing plays is like designing and building bridges. Like the bridge builder, you are involved in planning, designing, crafting, and constructing—in a very real sense plays are "built" more than "written"—and you focus on frame, shape, and style. Both playwright and bridge builder are visionaries, imagining a connection where none exists; both seek to take people where they've never been; both want the journey to stimulate the traveler's eye, mind, and spirit.

You face practical and aesthetic considerations as you design a construction that will take the traveler to the specific destination you've planned. You are necessarily deeply concerned about structural integrity—the nuts, bolts, and other devices that hold the whole together—but you want the traveler to experience the totality of the trip, not notice individual units. Your work may be straightforward and unobtrusive, a charming, small, covered bridge, or it may be a grand, dazzling, complex monument like the Golden Gate Bridge.

Just as there are many bridge designs, so plays can have various styles and approaches. More important, just as basic rules guide the construction of a bridge that will not collapse, so there are fundamental concepts involved in writing a play that will hold the stage. Learning those "rules" is an essential part of successful playwriting. Then you reshape and refashion styles and approaches to use or break the rules as you see fit.

The comparison of playwright with bridge builder goes further. A *playwright*, not *playwrite*, is involved in *playwriting*, not *playwrighting*. "Wright" suggests craftsmanship in construction, a hallmark of the successful playwright. The spelling parallels a *shipwright* who makes ships and a *wheelwright* who makes wheels. You bring to your writing a lively sense of construction for the stage.

BEING A PLAYWRIGHT MEANS WRITING STAGEWORTHY PLAYS, NOT "CLOSET DRAMAS"

You write plays that need theatre's magical alchemy to make their full impact. Directors look for stageworthy qualities in your play and reject it if they are absent. Although "stageworthy" is admittedly difficult to define because tastes, styles, and imaginations vary, here we introduce some of the basic qualities of a stageworthy play, and later chapters will examine the concept in more detail. You will develop personal ideas about stageworthiness as you continue studying the art of playwriting. We can start our definition by examining negative examples, plays that aren't stageworthy, often called "closet dramas."

What Is "Closet Drama"?

You may read some literary works that look like plays—they appear to be dialogues between individuals—but you sense they simply wouldn't work on stage. We call them closet dramas, an author's mental or stylistic exercise, more debates or excursions in language than dramatic action, and the opposite of a play meant for the stage. "Closet" in this sense refers to a small drawing room where literary people congregate. These nonplays are valuable negative examples that help you distinguish what is stageworthy.

Examples of closet dramas start with Plato, the Greek philosopher who wrote "Dialogues," apparently designed to be spoken but actually intellectual philosophical exercises best read privately. In his "Dialogues" you find individuals (one hesitates to call them characters) who have no emotional involvement or contact with the issues, and the dialogues are abstract debates without evolving and building action. The Roman playwright Seneca wrote "plays" such as *Octavia*, exercises that transform poorly to the stage because they use stereotypical heroines and heroes who only slightly resemble humans. They, too, debate each other without feeling, personal involvement, or concern about the outcome. Closet drama was especially popular during the Victorian age when poets wrote "dramas" that were stylistic exercises without dramatic action, perhaps best exemplified by Swinburne's *Chastelard* and *Mary Stuart*. Whatever the literary or intellectual merits of such closet dramas, they simply are not theatrical.

What Is a "Stageworthy" Play?

Unlike a closet drama, a play fulfills its author's purpose when it is staged, a process demanding active contributions from actors, director, designers, and audience. The play must be a passionate expression of the playwright's vision; conflict sparks action, which must be plausible and compelling; characters must be credible and dimensional with a life of their own; dialogue must be easily speakable by actors and instantly understandable by audiences; events must be compressed economically to achieve intensity; and the combined effects must flow from beginning to end. All achieve maximum impact when given life onstage.

Throughout this book we'll cite examples of stageworthy plays, noting that each must be staged for full effect because reading it silently to oneself in the privacy of one's home will diminish the work. We'll discuss how you write works for the live theatre using theme, conflict, action, language, voices of the performers, visual aspects of action, and characters' emotional involvement. The goal is to help you learn appropriate techniques so you can create equally stageworthy plays.

BEING A PLAYWRIGHT REQUIRES UNDERSTANDING— ALTHOUGH NOT ALWAYS FOLLOWING— RULES AND GUIDELINES

The idea of rules for playwrights or any other creative artist is controversial. Experienced playwrights urge new writers to "learn the rules before you break them." Beginners might insist, however, that an artist must have freedom to create without restrictions, and they reject rules on the belief that they are autocratic laws. Experienced writers see such active denial of advice, which is gained from hard experience, as a profitless expenditure of creative energy that could be better spent writing stageworthy plays that show the reasons rules exist.

Theatre is no different from other arts: Successful rule breakers are well known and often praised for their innovative contributions. A careful study of their plays, however, often leads to the conclusion that they broke few rules but instead adapted them for a fresh new style. We also might ask ourselves what the ratio is between successful rule breakers, whose plays are hailed as trailblazers opening new theatrical vistas, and those playwrights who broke rules and languish in obscurity, frustrated and lost, because their plays simply did not hold together or because their avoidance of rules created writing problems that prevented them from even finishing their works.

Try Rules Before You Reject Them

Perhaps the best advice about rules is simply, "Try them first before you reject them." No individual or group arbitrarily sets rules for playwrights. Instead, over time, empirical observation of plays—pragmatic theatre workers look for what works—has led to conclusions that create basic understandings about the shape and ingredients of a successful play.

Experienced playwrights recognize that there are a number of theatrical conventions, time-honored storytelling devices, which theatre personnel and audiences expect. These expectations, although not permanently engraved in granite, influence reactions to the playwright's work. Violating the conventions, while potentially exciting, can increase the risk that one's work will be ignored or misunderstood.

Remember that rules and guidelines exist not to inhibit your creative freedom but to help you channel your creative energies toward writing plays that have an improved chance of succeeding. If you give rules a fair trial but find they are worthless, you have grounds to discard them. If you find that they are helpful, however, you can adapt them to your own needs.

THEATRICAL DIRECTORS DESCRIBE WHAT THEY LOOK FOR IN PLAYS

As a director, deciding on whether to direct a play, I ask the following questions: Am I engaged by the play? Do I care about what the playwright cares about? Is his way of revealing what we both care about unique? Is his voice a valid one? Is the structure of the play essentially dramatic? Is the spine of the play—a complete story with revelation and conclusion—embedded in the material somehow?

LLOYD RICHARDS

[When I am deciding whether to direct a play] I look to see if the play is relevant in some particular way to life as the artist has experienced it.

MARSHALL W. MASON

The single quality that jumps out of every script I like is honesty. The kind of text that attracts me is one that comes right from the writer's gut. . . . I respond to writing that comes from the heart and isn't essentially literary.

ARVIN BROWN

BEING A PLAYWRIGHT MEANS WRITING, WRITING, AND WRITING

Writing is a difficult art to master, requiring devotion, study, and practice if one is to succeed. Of the various forms of writing, playwriting is the most difficult, according to well-known authors who have written both novels and plays, such as Thornton Wilder (whose novels and plays include, respectively, *The Bridge of San Luis Rey* and *Our Town*, both winners of Pulitzer Prizes) and James Kirkwood (known as a novelist for *Good Times/Bad Times*, as a playwright for *P.S. Your Cat Is Dead!*, and as one of the writers of *A Chorus Line*, for which he shared a Pulitzer Prize). Such writers say they find plays more difficult to write—as Wilder says, drama "is far harder than the novel"—and it follows that it requires of you even more devoted study, practice, and perseverance.

Write to Learn to Write

An essential step toward mastering the art and craft of playwriting is to convince yourself that above all else you *must* write. If you want to be a playwright, write. If you want to learn how to marry structure with content, write. If you want to find ideas, awaken your imagination, turn on your vision, sharpen your eye for people's hearts and your insight into their problems and struggles, understand yourself more clearly and sympathetically, and come to grips with what's most important to you in your corner of the world, you must write.

The Blank Page

The empty computer screen or blank sheet of paper is every writer's antagonist, creating barriers to the writer's goals as expertly as Iago to Othello's. This writer's nemesis is an opponent you must combat vigorously and earnestly, arm-wrestling it to defeat, prepared to struggle every day if necessary until you win.

On its side are all the old enemies, such as procrastination, hypercritical attitudes about your writing, self-induced doubts about the value of your basic idea, a hunger to achieve perfection but a paralyzing fear that you won't reach your goal, and substitution of other temporary goals that lead you to do *anything*—sharpen pencils, get coffee, clean closets, watch television, wash the dog, wax the car—rather than write. One writer wryly says her friends and relatives can tell when she's having trouble with her play because that's when her correspondence to them sharply increases.

Overcome the Blank Page

You're not alone when you have difficulties getting started: Every writer must fight to overcome self-defeatist attitudes. Believe you will win. On your side is your hunger to express yourself, love of writing and theatre, dedication to your goal, pride in accomplishment, sense of self-worth, dogged determination to prove to yourself you can succeed, and knowledge that even the largest project gets done one page at a time.

Overcome the blank page by seeing it as an opportunity, not an enemy: Convince yourself that empty space awaits your ideas, your vision, and your passion. Tell yourself that no blank piece of paper or empty computer screen can beat you, and right now you'll fill at least one page with parts of a play. When that page is completed, you'll do another page. Soon you'll have completed 4 pages. Write 4 pages a day for a month, and you'll finish 120 pages, the size of a full-length play.

Keep your expectations reasonable. Seek perfection, of course, but not all at once. First write your play, going from beginning to end, avoiding qualitative judgments while you're writing. Only after you've completed a first draft should you start demanding higher quality of your play and yourself, depending on the revision process (see Chapter 8) to improve your script.

It Must Come to "Writing Today"

> "The rule is, jam tomorrow, and jam yesterday—but never jam *today*."
> "It must come sometimes to 'jam today,'" Alice objected.
> "No, it can't," said the Queen. "It's jam every *other* day. Today isn't any *other* day, you know."

According to the Queen's wonderfully wacky Wonderland logic, Alice would never get any jam, and if the Queen's rules dictate a writer's life, he or she would never get anything written. As a playwright you convince yourself that if you want to write, it must come to writing today, not that other day that never comes.

The Serendipity Factor

Try to force yourself to write regularly, even if that means sitting at the keyboard and typing dialogue that has no connection with a known play. The point of this effort is partly to learn to think of writing as an active, not passive, searching process; and partly to encourage what can be called the "serendipity factor" or the ability to make desirable discoveries by apparent accident. The act of writing can help you make those fortunate discoveries that stimulate a flow of ideas for more writing.

You can test the validity of the serendipity factor with a simple experiment: Invent two characters, give them specific names, and make them begin talking about anything. Write as quickly as you can. The initial dialogue may appear pointless, but after a dozen pages the characters take on life and dimension and you'll begin to think of ways to place the characters in a more meaningful situation.

Such exercises show that the only way to write is simply to write and that nothing gets written while you wait for a flash of divine inspiration. On the other hand, creative ideas will come if you make a situation that encourages them. As has been frequently observed, "writing is nine-tenths perspiration and one-tenth inspiration." Convince yourself that only writing produces writing.

PLAYWRIGHTS DESCRIBE THEIR WORK HABITS

I find it almost impossible to write any time but in the morning, when I have more energy to write. . . . I am a compulsive writer. I have tried to stop working and I am bored to death. . . . It takes a physical toll of your nervous energies. You've got to do all kinds of things to try to make yourself stand up under it.

TENNESSEE WILLIAMS

I write the first draft in longhand in an exercise book. I type the second—making changes in the process—and then go over it with a pen before retyping it again. There may be any number of drafts before I'm satisfied.

ARNOLD WESKER

I'm usually up around six, and I'm almost always at the typewriter by eight and I write until twelve or one, usually.

WILLIAM INGE

SPECIAL ADVANTAGES OF BEING A PLAYWRIGHT

You'll find that being a playwright brings both challenges and advantages. The challenges often appear overwhelming. There'll be times you aren't sure you'll win the battle of marrying form, structure, characterization, and dialogue to express your vision. On the other hand, one major advantage is the feeling of accomplishment when you create a work of art. Each victory will sustain you through future struggles.

The Excitement of Playwriting

Theatre's impact on others. Through theatre you have a remarkable oportunity to influence audiences. Many examples could be cited, but perhaps one of the more striking is described by playwright Arthur Miller in *Timebends: A Life.*

> As sometimes happened later on during the run, there was no applause at the final curtain of the first performance [of *Death of a Salesman*]. Strange things began to go on in the audience. With the curtain down, some people stood to put their coats on and then sat again, some, especially men, were bent forward covering their faces, and others were openly weeping. People crossed the theatre to stand quietly talking with one another. It seemed forever before someone remembered to applaud, and then there was no end to it. I was standing at the back and saw a distinguished-looking elderly man being led up the aisle; he was talking excitedly into the ear of what seemed to be his male secretary or assistant. This, I learned, was Bernard Gimbel, head of the department store chain, who that night gave an order that no one in his stores was to be fired for being overage.

Being a playwright is a deeply satisfying way to communicate your ideas to others, as Miller did, perhaps changing their perception of their actions. Writing plays can be—must be—a personally enriching experience. It also can be remarkably educational: Writing plays, especially creating characters, will give you increased sensitivity and insight into others. And into yourself.

EXERCISES

Each chapter concludes with exercises that will help you develop your art and craft. Always *write* your responses—you are, after all, a writer—and give yourself ample time to do each exercise thoroughly.

Record answers to these and other exercises in your personal *Playwright's Journal*, a large, three-ring notebook with a number of tab dividers for various categories such as "Play in Progress," "Next Play," "Daily Journal," "Calendar and Writing Schedule," "Dialogue," "Situations," "Diary of Writing," "Ideas for Plays," "Newspaper and Magazine Clippings," "Inspirational Quotations," "Exercises," and the like.

1. What are the strongest inner beliefs that control your being? What most awakes your interest? First list your beliefs, the topics that you care about more than any others, and then write about your feelings for each. Think of your statements as deeply personal expressions; no one will evaluate your answers, and there is no right or wrong response except that you should express your own sense of truth. Write several pages about each passion. Your detailed statements will become materials for plays you'll write.
2. What human traits do you value because you think they are praiseworthy? List them. What actions show those values? Give illustrations.
3. What personality traits strike you as negative? List them. Describe actions that show those qualities.
4. Make a list of stageworthy plays you've seen in production. Although it is difficult to isolate the playscript from the production, try to focus on the play itself, not actors, directors, or designers.
5. Using that list, describe why those plays held the stage. What made them work? What qualities appear essential for a play to work onstage? How did those plays grasp audience attention? Did you perceive a playwright's passion? What in the play's action attracted you? What aspects of characterization were most interesting? How does dialogue contribute to making a play stageworthy?

6. Schedule your writing time. At what hours will you write? For how long? How many days a week? Construct a calendar that assigns you specific writing periods.
7. Decide how you'll measure your writing period. Will you write a specific number of hours? Or will you write until you've completed a minimum number of pages? Write your assignment on your calendar.

Each morning my characters
greet me with misty faces
willing, though chilled, to muster
for another day's progress
through the dazzling quicksand
the marsh of blank paper.
　　　　　—John Updike

How can you write if you can't cry?
　　　　　—Ring Lardner

2

What Makes a Play?

The fantastic thing about the theatre is that it can make something be seen that's invisible, and that's where my interest in theatre is—that you can be watching this thing happening with actors and costumes and light and set and language, and even plot, and something emerges from beyond that, and that's the image part that I'm looking for, that sort of added dimension.

SAM SHEPARD

Being a playwright requires a sensitivity to the special demands of theatre, finding answers to the question, "What makes a play?" For theatrical writing *construction* is important because in a real sense plays are built as much as written. Continued experience writing plays, plus reading and seeing other playwrights' works, will help you establish personal concepts of what makes a play, especially what creates a good play.

This chapter focuses on the elements that make a play, helping you transform your ideas from rough form into a theatrical work. In particular we look at basic concepts of stageworthy plays, helping you write plays that will satisfy producers, directors, and actors, thus giving you a better chance of being produced. No single definition of a play can satisfy all playwrights, but you'll find that certain basic qualities are essential regardless of genre, form, length, or other aspects of writing.

DEFINITION OF A PLAY

A play is a structured and unified story, comic or dramatic, complete in itself with a beginning, middle, and end, that expresses the playwright's passion and vision of life, shows unfolding conflict that builds to a climax, and deals with dimensional lifelike humans who have strong emotions, needs, and objectives that motivate them to take action. It is constructed with a plausible and probable series of events, written to be performed and therefore told with speeches and actions plus silences and inactions, projected by actors from a stage to an audience that is made to believe the events are happening as they watch.

A play deals with materials that "simply cannot be expressed by any other means," according to Eugène Ionesco, and it is constructed with "a complexity of words, movements, gestures that convey a vision of the world unexpressible in any other way." As Sam Shepard says, theatre transforms the invisible into the visible. It can be—many argue it must be—more magical than any other form of writing.

A PLAY IS NOT A NOVEL

In some respects you are like the novelist, poet, essayist, newspaper reporter, screenwriter, or even sermon writer. You share with them passion and commitment to writing, special delight in words and ideas, need to express a personal vision, fascination with the mysteries of human behavior, misgivings about social or political trends, dedication to self-improvement, ability to work long solitary hours, hunger for perfection, self-discipline that focuses your time and energy on your projects, and undefinable joy when you see your work in print or, in your case, on stage. You are driven by a compulsion to use your art to make connections between what others know and see, and an invisible unknown that only you envision.

A Play Is a Blueprint for Actors and Directors

More enlightening than similarities, however, are the differences between playwriting and all other forms of writing. Unlike the novelist, whose final product is a set form that is captured forever within the covers of a book, your play is interpreted and extended by talented directors, designers, and actors who dedicate their talents to bringing your play to life. With each new production your play is reborn, surprisingly different because of theatrical creativity and interpretation. In this sense your play is a blueprint designed for theatre personnel, and you write a stageworthy play by remaining keenly aware of their needs and their methods of communicating your play to an audience.

A Play Speaks to a Group Consciousness

Novelists write for one reader at a time; you write for a group consciousness. The novel's reader, if confused, can back up pages or even chapters to reread illuminating passages; your play must maintain an instant clarity so the audience member will have no questions about the facts. Novelists expect that a reader will put down the book for a period of time; you must grasp the audience's full, uninterrupted attention during the entire play.

Think of performances you've seen that captivated audiences throughout. What were the factors that caused the audience to concentrate on the play? As you remember such plays, quite likely you will recall the projection of strong emotions, conflicts between intriguing characters who were deeply involved in the action, the examination of significant issues, suspense and concern for the outcome, and crisp dialogue.

Plays Communicate with Dialogue and Action

A novelist or short story writer often uses expository passages to describe the environment, events, scenery, characters, characters' thoughts and feelings, and the like. Playwrights do not. You focus on what characters say and refuse to say, plus actions they do and do not take—all communications to the audience. Novelists or sermon writers can directly state moral points or lessons, but playwrights communicate such information only indirectly, using dialogue and actions.

Shakespeare's *Macbeth*, for example, has powerful actions that convey the play's thematic core about the destructiveness of a quest for absolute power. Imagine a novelist's version of the same story—expository passages describing Macbeth's inner core and hungers, his environment, choices, and, ultimately, the reasons for his downfall. In contrast, imagine a stage production with Macbeth showing his tension and conflict, the sounds of the language, the sweep of color and movement, and a sense of seeing action happening now.

Plays Are Set in the Present, Moving to a Future

Present tense. Characters in a novel *did* or *said* this or that; in a play the characters *are doing* action and *are speaking* dialogue *now*. The distinction is vital. A novel is written in the past tense, relating events that took place and were completed before the reader picked up the book; your play lives in a perpetual present tense, depicting events that are unfolding this very moment in front of the audience.

Future tense. If the present tense distinguishes a play from a novel, a sense of impending future distinguishes a play with dramatic impact from a nondramatic script. Your play's characters and actions have a lively, ever-present sense of future. The current actions of a play's characters must constantly move toward some impending goal; plays must have forward-looking action; present actions must convey potential consequences.

Present and future tense requirements of a playwright. If you find that your characters continually refer to past events, ask yourself if you should reset your play in that past situation. Equally, if your characters seem to lack interest in the future, ask if you should recreate them to have specific goals that are highly important to them. As we discuss in later chapters, sensitivity to your characters' present and future will greatly ease problems when constructing plot and motivating characters.

Plays' Movement in Time and Place

Novels, like screenplays, are enhanced by frequent and sweeping movements through time and space. Plays, on the other hand, are more powerful when tightly written. Novels often seek to depict a large number of scenes to show the story's large universe; plays compress action into one whole that represents that larger universe. One appeal of a novel is its ability to view life through a wide-angle, even panoramic, lens. Your play, however, gains strength with a more narrow focus on specific actions that are most significant to your vision.

Plays Show, Not Tell

A play must show what characters are thinking and feeling; a novel may *tell* and describe (although most novelists adapt the "show, not tell" concept to various degrees). A novelist may editorialize explicitly about concepts regarding life or the novel's meaning; you communicate the same concepts but only through actions, not direct statements. A novelist can describe what characters are thinking; you must show what characters are thinking by their actions and inactions, speeches and silences. You work on the time-honored premise that "actions speak louder than words" to show the play's thought and the characters' goals and emotions.

The Play's Objective and Collective Point of View

Fiction writers may choose to write from a character's viewpoint, how that character sees events. They may, for example, use an omniscient point of view to relate any character's perception, a first-person view that uses the word *I* to take the reader into the mind of the major character, or a third-person viewpoint that does not use the word *I* but otherwise focuses on what one character feels, believes, hears, and sees.

Playwrights, in contrast, write with an objective and collective point of view. You represent all characters—one way of writing plays is to "become" each character while he or she is speaking and reacting—and you seek to show each character's individual attitudes, emotions, goals, hopes, and dreams.

Plays Are Written for Actors to Communicate to the Audience's Eye and Ear

A stageworthy play is written for actors to speak and do. The novelist expects readers will enjoy perfectly constructed and balanced sentences, reread favorite passages, look up unfamiliar words, or check a literary concordance to find sources of allusions to poems or other forms of literature. In contrast, your audiences respond to the overall action and characterization in movement, not to individual literary moments. Passages that call attention to themselves in a play are considered distracting and therefore are seldom acceptable. Audiences must be able to understand words and references immediately, requiring you to craft dialogue that makes things clear by context.

A Play Faces Added Revisions

Novelists, short story authors, and other writers are finished when their projects are accepted by a publisher, although some rewriting may be necessary. In contrast, the playwright faces more revisions, seeking clarity, structural strength, action, depth of characterization, and lively dialogue. Many such aspects of your play are tested by the crucible of performance, and a play that looks correct on paper may turn out to need major or minor changes when theatre personnel begin bringing it to life. Once your script is accepted by a producer or director, you should expect to continue making major revisions during rehearsals while the play is being put on its feet, and yet again after judging audience reaction to your play.

PLAYS REQUIRE CONFLICT

Novels may succeed without conflict. Not plays. Conflict is so essential for effective plays that a "law of conflict" is a recognized permanent part of successful theatrical writing. Conflict is the motor that propels your play forward. Without conflict there is no movement, no issues, no questions raised and examined, no character changes in response to stimuli, and no suspense to hold audience attention. Conflict creates the dramatic tension necessary for any play, comic or tragic. A play without conflict is, simply, a play without dramatic impact.

Conflict Is Force Against Force

Conflict most typically is one individual (protagonist) seeking a goal (objective) but opposed by comparable force (one or more antagonists). Stated most simply, conflict is boy (protagonist) highly motivated to want girl (objective) but confronted with parents (antagonists) who violently oppose the match. This particular model has had countless successful retellings in theatre literature, perhaps most notably in *Romeo and Juliet* and *West Side Story*. But the model isn't restricted to boy-wants-girl or even love: Variations of that basic structure are found in countless other successful plays that deal with quite different plots, themes, and characters but nonetheless are built with a protagonist seeking a goal and facing strong opposition. The result is conflict.

Think of the basic protagonist-goal versus antagonist-opposition outline as a skeleton that you can use to create numerous other dramatic conflicts. To that framework you add flesh, intellect, emotion, and meaning by investing your unique vision, beliefs, and voice, turning the framework into your own original statement.

Opposing Forces Have Equal Strengths

Opposing forces must be equal, or else the play's action cannot be sustained. The zeal of the parental objections must match the boy's fervor for the girl, and the balance of power continually shifts, as in a prizefight, during the course of the play. First one force appears to win, then the other. One force may doubt the wisdom of the action, creating internal conflict; another force may call in outside reinforcements. There are reversals and discoveries; obstacles are encountered, destroyed, and reborn. The intensity of the struggle grows as each side senses victory. These shifts in balance create suspense, compelling the audience to concentrate on your play.

Conflict Expresses the Play's Meaning

How do you communicate the play's overall intellectual meaning if you can't use didactic speeches that state the questions, solution, and concept? Through action. What the characters *do* indicates the play's core question and the playwright's vision of answers to dilemmas.

Playwrights often tackle ethical issues, changing abstract questions into concrete human terms. Many illustrations could be cited, but we mention only a few here:

- We must keep clear the distinction between justice and revenge: *Medea* by Euripides.
- One should not value money as highly as people: *The Miser* by Molière.
- A woman must have the right to be respected as a person: *A Doll's House* by Henrik Ibsen.
- The Holocaust was a dreadful tragedy that destroyed humans and major human values: *The Investigation* by Peter Weiss.

In all such plays, the moral lesson is not verbalized but is shown through conflict.

Conflict and Abstract Forces

Conflict can involve the individual against abstract forces, such as self or society, but because drama requires showing instead of telling, such conflict is effective only when that abstraction is made concrete by one or more specific characters in the play. For example, on one level *Hamlet* involves internal conflict, Hamlet against himself, but that is shown through the external conflicts between Hamlet and Claudius and Gertrude. Those external conflicts illuminate the internal struggles Hamlet experiences.

Conflict Creates Dimensional Characters

Conflict enhances characterization because struggles show characters in changing mental and emotional sets; without struggles, characters would remain the same. Each twist and turn of the conflict makes characters find new ways to deal with new situations, thus showing new dimensional qualities. Characters would lack motivation to change without those variations that result from conflict's struggles. As the balance of power shifts, characters necessarily must respond to stimuli; without stimuli, the characters would not change. Struggle makes characters become more dimensional and interesting.

Conflict Provides the Structure of the Play

Plot is more easily understood when you think of it as the structure of conflict. Drama is the art of the showdown, conflict in action, the play's characters at work in the present to achieve a goal in the future while attempting to overcome conflicts such as obstacles, reversals, and complications. *Hamlet* contains a number of showdown scenes, such as between Hamlet and the Ghost, Hamlet and Gertrude, Hamlet and his uncle, and Hamlet and Laertes.

The sequential order of conflict makes up the structure of plot. A given play's plot begins with an initial conflict, which sparks the protagonist into the action that makes up the core plot; the middle contains the building struggles that develop the plot; and the end resolves that conflict. Without conflict there is neither plot nor structure.

Conflict draws the audience into the play, making them involved in the action; and conflict provides a sense of momentous events in progress in contrast to a sense that "nothing happens." The audience is fascinated by the effects of the conflict on the characters, empathizing with struggles to overcome crises, problems, emergencies, and complications. A play such as *Romeo and Juliet*, for example, has a strong appeal based on the conflicts that the lovers encounter in pursuit of happiness.

SELECTIVITY: DRAMA IS AN INTERPRETATION OF LIFE, NOT REAL LIFE

Imagine a large party, a familiar real-life situation. Everybody's talking at once, music is blaring, people are milling about. In the middle of the chaos, two people are having a violent argument. Others watch or perhaps leave. Some get drunk and begin to sing. Imagine the playwright tape-records the party. Can the affair be transcribed word for word and made into a play?

Or imagine two people arriving at a restaurant. They are led to a table. They sit. They chat. Someone takes their order. They continue to chat while they wait for dinner. Drinks arrive. They chat. They wait. Dinner arrives. They chat while they eat. Again, this is real life, but can it be transcribed into a play?

In both instances the answer is, "Not likely." The playwright interested in dramatizing those scenes would have to make choices, a process of selectivity that is a vital part of art: finding a way to represent those aspects that appear most important and that can be shaped into dramatic action.

Plays are based on life and show your vision of reality, but they are never real life. Instead, plays are artistic representations of the playwright's concept of certain aspects of life. You *select* from life. This distinction can help you understand the need to shape materials in a way that permits dramatization.

If you want to write about the party, for example, you must select the most important events and shape the action to make it dramatic. You might decide to place the party offstage to permit focus on the arguing couple. Alternatively, you might start the play an hour or so after the party, assume the couple has just arrived home, and dramatize the couple's argument.

PLAYS ARE COMPLETE IN THEMSELVES

A play is a holistic communication, complete in itself and containing all necessary information. It cannot depend on clarification from external sources such as announcements or notes in programs given audiences, author's explanations, or audience knowledge of other plays, novels, or contemporary or historical events. Explanatory footnotes and stage directions, while certainly useful to production personnel, are not communicated to audiences.

PLAYS HAVE A BEGINNING, MIDDLE, AND END

A play must have a beginning, middle, and end. Although this advice appears elemental, adherence to it can help solve any structural problem that may arise. You may have seen plays that jumped into action so quickly, you felt confused by the lack of an orientation to the characters or situation; and you've probably seen plays that seemed to stop rather than end. Such plays illustrate the need for a beginning and an end. You may also have seen plays that begin examining a major question, then suddenly wrap up the pieces and end too quickly, without probing the question in sufficient detail. Such plays illustrate the need for a sustained middle.

The beginning, middle, and end should be artistically balanced, admittedly a rather vague and subjective term. That requirement is helpful but defies exact specification because you are writing a play, not following a recipe for a soufflé. The point is that you give each portion its due, and it can help to think of these three parts as the protagonist's movements. At the beginning he or she starts a major action, motivated to achieve a goal. During the middle the protagonist struggles to achieve that purpose. At the end he or she succeeds or fails, and in the process that character, or possibly one or more other characters, gains a new insight, which the audience also perceives.

The content and structure of the play will dictate how much importance is placed on each of these three elements. No one wishes to tell you that the beginning must be fifteen percent of the whole, the middle has to be seventy percent and the ending will be fifteen percent, but those percentages at least suggest the relative importance of each part of the triad. Note that the middle dominates because it contains action, movements of the plot, and development of the characters, which all add up to communicate the play's basic meaning.

AVOID CINEMATIC WRITING

> *One of the litmus tests of a good play is that it is not a television script in disguise. I think, "Could this only work in the theater? Could this be better done as a movie with close-ups and angles, or not?" I think theater should stick with what it and nothing else can provide: language, imagination, dream.*
>
> —Eric Overmyer

Many modern theatrical directors are distressed by plays characterized by loose cinematic writing, with style and technique more appropriate for television or motion pictures than for the theatre. Such scripts typically have numerous brief scenes, often with no beginning, middle, or end, and many episodic jumps in time and space. Avoiding cinematic writing improves your chances for production of your play.

Danger Signals of Cinematic Writing

Learn to recognize certain danger flags signaling cinematic thinking that may permeate your play. For example, you're thinking of a camera's dolly movement if your play starts with the characters, say, walking through a mall, entering a shop to browse, and picking up small items the audience must see. You're thinking of a camera's zoom lens if the audience is to see a small property, such as the contents of a letter, or if the audience is to recognize a character's emotions by "a glint in her eye." More dangerous, because corrective revision can be difficult, you're thinking of cinematic storytelling techniques if your play makes frequent jumps in time and space or demands large-scale physical activity.

Movies and television tell stories more with visual qualities and less with dialogue, the opposite of stage writing. Screenwriters talk about "opening up" a story by including more characters and scenes, as illustrated by movie adaptations of plays; playwrights intensify the story by focusing on fewer characters and only the most essential locales. Movies are at their best with large, sweeping physical action, illustrated by motion pictures such as *Alien* and *Raiders of the Lost Ark*. Plays are at their best when focused on psychological action, such as *A Streetcar Named Desire* and *Who's Afraid of Virginia Woolf?*

DRAMATIC ACTION MUST BE POSSIBLE, PLAUSIBLE, AND PROBABLE

A play must be true to its own logic, which starts by establishing its ground rules or universe in the opening action. That logic cannot be violated later. A play can deal successfully with imaginative fantasy, science fiction projections into the future, or other materials not found in the logical, objective, real world, such as flying fairies (*Peter Pan*), robots (*R. U. R.*), space travel (*Night of the Auk*), or a man with a six-foot-tall, invisible rabbit friend (*Harvey*), but only if action is possible, plausible, and probable within the universe the play creates.

Surprise and mystery are vital components in a play, but not at the expense of the play's own ground rules. For example, unlikely to be plausible, probable, and possible would be a play with a realistic universe that introduces problems that are solved in the last minutes by the surprise appearance of fairies or an invisible rabbit, because they were not part of the play's initial logic.

PLAYS ARE ENTERTAINMENT

From the first it has been theatre's business to entertain people as it also has been of all the other arts. It is this business which gives it its particular dignity; it needs no other passport but fun.

—Bertolt Brecht

Some scoff at the idea of theatre as entertainment, as if that somehow cheapens the art or makes it into a meringue-filled confection without intellectual substance. In fact, however, to entertain is a respectable and vital aspect of theatre. Those who deny the concept of theatre as entertainment are likely the same people, playwrights and directors, whose theatrical work is self-indulgent, pompous, dull, and noncommunicative, making audiences walk out during performances.

The definition of a play includes the audience; the concept of entertainment is a sensible extension of that definition. A play captures and holds the audience's attention only if it entertains, by which is meant "to divert from daily, mundane concerns." It follows that both *King Lear* and *The Sound of Music* are entertainment. Both are compelling and well-structured stories that stimulate audiences to concentrate on the action; both are rich in plausible conflict, move toward a future that deeply affects the characters, contain surprise and mystery, have interesting and dimensional characters who face problems that are made significant to their future, contain well-written dialogue, and lift the audience members out of themselves into the universe of the play. As playwrights such as George Bernard Shaw have proved, entertaining plays can provoke audiences to respond thoughtfully to important social or other intellectual issues.

PLAYS COMMUNICATE WITH EMOTIONS

Not all guidelines are acceptable to everyone, and certainly there are several schools of thought regarding the importance of emotion. Some argue that plays communicate to the audience's intellect when emotions are evoked. On the other hand, some echo Plato's belief, later reinforced by Bertolt Brecht's concept of "epic theatre," that audiences stop thinking when emotional. (It should be pointed out that even Brecht's plays do use emotional appeal, although he sometimes includes scenes or effects that briefly cancel emotional response.) In any case, wisdom points out that it is senseless to treat emotions and intellect like two unrelated parts of the human response. In fact, they cannot be separated.

Many theatre workers believe that plays are enhanced when characters have reason to experience strong emotions such as love and hate; the weaker versions such as "like a little" or "sort of dislike" are as unsatisfactory as musical minor chords. Without adequate motivation those emotions may degrade to soap opera qualities, but we can safely say that when characters care deeply about the issues and problems they face, the audience also will care, through the process of empathy. Not unimportant for the playwright, actors are apt to become more involved with characters who experience emotional ranges, resulting in powerful interpretations of a play.

PLAYS COMMUNICATE TO THE IMAGINATION

Producers, directors, actors, and designers seek plays that leap off the page to the stage, awakening their theatrically trained imaginations to "see" and "hear" the characters and action. Audiences also respond positively to plays that communicate to the imagination, forcing them to participate in the play and empathize with the characters.

Too much detail inhibits imaginative responses, and a primary aspect of playwriting is deciding what to omit or exclude, achieving a balance of mystery with essential clarity. Audiences at a production of *Harvey* readily "see" Harvey through the character's eyes, and the effect would be markedly lessened if a six-foot actor played the role in a bunny suit. Your study of plays such as Harold Pinter's *The Dumbwaiter* and Samuel Beckett's *Waiting for Godot* will help you discover the value of encouraging imaginative response by deciding what *not* to write.

UNITIES OF TIME, PLACE, AND ACTION

The so-called Aristotelian three unities—so-called because they are inaccurately derived from Aristotle's *Poetics*—supposedly require a play to be consistent in time, place, and action. The concept can be confusing because many playwriting textbooks and play directors recommend you follow the unities carefully, but some playwrights and directors tell you to disregard the unities completely. Neither extreme is correct.

The unities have a certain logic. Unity of time means that a play's action happens in twenty-four hours or less; unity of place holds the action to a single locale, such as one room; and unity of action (the unity suggested by Aristotle) requires the play to dramatize only one central story or action, which eliminates action not directly relevant to the plot.

These unities often are misunderstood, and we mustn't exaggerate their significance although we must recognize that they can contribute to a play's impact. A playwright has a certain amount of freedom to ignore them, but that freedom isn't absolute. Their importance warrants your study so you can decide when and how to apply the unities to your play.

Historical Obedience to
Unities of Time, Place, and Action

Rigid observance of the unities of time, place, and action is found in various centuries of theatre's development. For one example,

Ludovico Castelvetro, the sixteenth-century Italian poet and critic, initiated the concept of "unity of time," basing his conclusions on a passage from Aristotle's *Poetics* that compares epic poetry and tragedy. (The former, Aristotle wrote, does not need to follow a unity of time, but the latter "endeavors, as far as possible, to confine itself to a single revolution of the sun.")

Castelvetro's concept grew in importance to the point that some Renaissance theorists demanded that "stage time" be congruent with "real time," by which they meant that any real-life action that requires, say, twenty minutes should take precisely the same amount of time on stage. These and comparable rules, known as "neoclassical ideals," permeated much of the Renaissance. Modern theatre, however, is less rigid.

Modern Theatrical Use of the Unities

Today's theatre rejects compulsive observance of the unities on the justifiable grounds that, first, they are based on misreading Aristotle's *Poetics*. Second, portions—not all—of the rules of unities are artificial. Finally, effective contemporary plays prove that the unities are guides, not dictates.

Time and place. The unities of time and place often are discarded in today's plays, although unity of action continues to be important. Modern use of the unities may be best exemplified by free-flowing plays such as Arthur Miller's *Death of a Salesman*, which moves easily through time and space, most notably with the appearance of Ben, who exists only in Willy's imagination. You can better understand the effect of rigid insistence on unity of time and place by imagining *Salesman* if Miller had confined his play to one time and place. The character of Ben would be eliminated, thus sharply decreasing the portrayal of Willy; and scenes such as Willy with the whore would not be possible, thereby excluding a vital aspect of the Willy-Biff conflict.

Freedom to ignore unities of time and place is accompanied by a need to structure the play tightly, and you must know the chronological order of the action, no matter what unities are shown in the play. We can return to *Salesman* to illustrate this point. Although a casual observer might conclude that Miller's play lacks unification of time because the play shows a number of scenes from Willy Loman's past, in fact *Salesman* has a strong unification of time that is often overlooked: The action deals with the last forty-eight hours of Willy's life.

That observer might say those Willy-Ben or Willy-whore scenes in *Salesman* are flashbacks, but it is more accurate to think of them as insights into moments that are engraved in Willy's mind and make him the man who is dissolving in the present. Miller says his play has no flashbacks but "it is simply that the past keeps flowing into the present, bringing its scenes and its characters with it." Miller doesn't distinguish when those moments happened— there's no chronological specificity—but they clearly show young Willy Loman's warped values that lead to his suicide.

Action. Although modern plays effectively ignore unities of time and place, they continue to emphasize unity of action because the alternative could be chaotic. Without a clear unification of action, plays can be so disconnected that they lose clarity and impact. Too many plots results in a lack of emphasis. Certainly *Salesman* has one basic action: Willy's (unsuccessful) efforts to make Biff love him, resulting in his self-destruction.

Unity of action is most important to the playwright. Of the three unities, action is the one that should most concern you. Unity of action, most easily defined as a single, organic plot, is an important structural device to make your play dramatic by maintaining a logical connection between successive events. Unity of action gives strength to such diverse plays as Henrik Ibsen's *Ghosts*, Sam Shepard's *Fool for Love*, and Neil Simon's *Broadway Bound*.

Advantages of Observing the Unities

Value of the unities. Although effective plays disregard certain unities, you should recognize the advantages of observing them. One cardinal precept of art is that there must be an underlying unification to the work, a glue that holds all parts together. One technique—certainly not the only way—is through the use of the three unities, and often your play has a stronger chance of being better written, more intense, and stageworthy if you unify time, place, and action. Short monodramas and one-act plays, in particular, usually follow the three unities. Furthermore, observation of the three unities helps you avoid numerous pitfalls lurking to trap the playwright who too freely disregards them; following the unities can help you write more easily.

These advantages do not mean that you must slavishly follow

the unities, but they are so significant that beginning playwrights should seriously consider making their first plays unified in time, place, and action. The same advice is valid for advanced writers who have not written a play containing these unities or who are frustrated by problems on a current script.

Tips for Effective Use of the Unities

Plausibility. Applying a rule of plausibility will help you avoid common pitfalls with time. Avoid calling audience attention to illogical passage of time, such as having a character consume an alcoholic drink on page four and become drunk by page six; sending a character offstage, saying he's going to get a sandwich at the corner deli, only to return with the sandwich on the next page or so; or having an offstage character telephone to say she's on her way over, and then appear on stage within several minutes. Be careful, too, about sending one character offstage to shower or change clothing, which requires a certain passage of time, leaving the other character onstage with nothing to say or do.

Scenery shifts for time or place are distracting. If you elect to shift time or place during the course of your play, consider making the shifts flow in nonstop action. Stage machinery, no matter how smoothly handled, interrupts the action and disrupts audience concentration. Breaks for scenery shifts to indicate change in time or place are awkward unless done during an intermission.

A careful study of plays that successfully move in time and place will help you better perceive the necessary writing techniques. We've already cited *Salesman* as a model. A second excellent example is *Canadian Gothic*, a powerful one-act by Joanna Glass, which flows freely in time and place without interruption or changes in setting, skillfully using direct address and narration so the audience is never in doubt. Undoubtedly you can find more.

THE FOURTH (AND MOST IMPORTANT) UNITY: PLAYWRIGHT'S PURPOSE

Centuries of controversy regarding unities of time, place, and action have overshadowed attention to a more important unification: the playwright's purpose or passion, the spark that gives birth to the writer's germinal idea, the playwright's need to bring to theatrical life a situation, issue, or character that illustrates the writer's deepest inner concerns. Strangely, texts on playwriting ignore unification by playwright's purpose.

Your play will be unified when you know clearly what you want to write and have a definite passion or idea you must communicate. Conversely, plays become murky or confusing when the writer loses sight of the passion that started the writing process. Loss of that vision can result in a play that appears to be two or three plays uncomfortably lumped together.

As you begin thinking of a play that wants to be written, continually ask yourself questions to clarify your goal: "What do I want to say?" "What ideas or characters do I want to dramatize?" "What's this play all about?" Answers to such questions might be posted on the bulletin board over your writing area, and you may want to glance at them as you first outline and then write your play.

EXERCISES

These exercises will help you think of ways to turn an idea into a stageworthy play. Record answers in your writer's notebook.

1. Imagine you are commissioned to adapt your favorite novel for the stage. Write an outline of any scenes you wish. What changes will you make? In what time and place will you set the action? How will you reduce the number of characters? What will you do to tighten the time? How will you decrease the number of locations? Will you attempt to dramatize the entire novel, or parts? How will you decide? What do you conclude are significant differences between a novel and a play?
2. Select your favorite play and write a brief outline showing how you would make it into a novel.
3. Assume you are commissioned to change your favorite movie into a stage play. Apply the questions from number 1 above to your process. Write a brief outline of any scenes you wish. What do you learn about the differences between cinematic and theatrical writing?
4. Turn your attention to a play you want to write. Write a brief synopsis that details the play's conflict. Answer questions such as the following:

What does the protagonist want? Be sure that goal is concrete and attainable through active motion. "To find happiness through love," for example, is too abstract, but "to marry Juliet" is playable.

Why? What makes that goal important?

Why is the protagonist motivated into action *now*?

What obstacles stop him or her from achieving that goal? The longer your play, the more obstacles you'll need. List them in order.

How does the character respond to those obstacles?

In your synopsis indicate how the conflicts and action reflect and show the play's content.

5. Write a brief summation of the action and contents of the beginning, middle, and end of the play you want to write.

A play's an interpretation. It is not a report. And that is the beginning of its poetry because, in order to interpret, you have to distort toward a symbolic construction of what happened, and as that distortion takes place, you begin to leave out and overemphasize and consequently deliver up life as a unity rather than as a chaos, and any such attempt, the more intense it is, the more poetic it becomes.

—Arthur Miller

Why do I write at all? There are things that concern me enough to compel the sustained committed effort that leads to the script of a play. I once told a friend in London that my plays are efforts to continue—and perhaps win—certain arguments that I've had with people. And, of course, the plays are about people and relationships—troubled relationships that seem to demand explaining.

—Arnold Wesker

3

The Size of Your Canvas: Monodramas, One-Acts, and Full-Length Plays

Writing has laws of perspective, of light and shade, just as painting does. . . . If you are born knowing them, fine. If not, learn them. Then rearrange the rules to suit yourself.

TRUMAN CAPOTE

Playwriting involves filling theatrical time and space, which refers to the length of your script and the action that happens onstage during that period. Length and action match each other—the longer your play, the more complex the action; the smaller the action, the shorter your play—and they combine to attract the audience's attention and awaken its imagination.

Your decisions about time and space are like the painter's choice of canvas size, as large or small as necessary to express your ideas. The painter might start with a vision of a sweeping city scene that demands a huge mural, or may first decide to paint a miniature and then select a subject that fits within those confines. Your creative process, like the painter's, includes determining the dimensions of your canvas, basing your decision on either your play's content or your target size.

DETERMINING THE SIZE OF YOUR CANVAS

Your canvas may be relatively small, like a brief one-person monodrama, or increasingly larger, ranging from a one-act to a full-length play. The colors of your canvas evoke the mood you wish—comic, dramatic, or tragic—and you shape the total effect so it communicates to a particular audience that you identify (thinking of age, locale, theatrical sophistication, and so on) at a specific theatre (such as professional, regional, educational, and so forth).

How Do You Decide the Size of Your Play?

You might determine your play's dimensions by first evaluating the scope of your basic germinal idea, involving such matters as the complexity of the plot and quantity of incidents, number of characters, physical settings, movement in time or space, and the development of the story. The more complex—the more elbow room you need—the larger your play. Alternatively, you may reverse the process and first select the length and complexity you wish to make your play, then select materials appropriate for that space. A third process, equally valid, is more exploratory: sketching out your play until you discover what size you'll need.

Size of Play Doesn't Equate with Importance

Avoid mistaken concepts that one size canvas is somehow more artistic or significant than another or that "serious" writers tackle only full-length plays because any other size indicates a lack of artistic ambition. Equally, don't let other people push you into those traps, as happened to a promising young playwright who was leaving the theatre following a production of her successful one-act play when a theatre professor said in a patronizing way, "That was nice. But when are you going to write a full-length *real* play?" His narrow-minded question threw her badly off stride, and her writing suffered for several years before she was able to recover her belief in her work.

Protect yourself by vigorously rejecting such poor, even cruel, advice. If you decide to write a short play, keep in mind the opinion of the late Alan Schneider, one of America's outstanding theatrical directors who was responsible for successful Broadway productions of playwrights such as Edward Albee and Samuel Beckett. "I like the short play," he said. "My grandmother taught me that diamonds don't come as large as bricks." Your goal is to select a canvas that expresses your deeply held personal beliefs and vision, following playwright Edward Albee's statement that "it is a playwright's responsibility to reflect and comment on his time as accurately as he possibly can."

THE MONODRAMA

As the name implies, a monodrama is a one-character play. Also known as a theatrical monologue, one-person show, or (in an evocation of vaudeville) a solo turn, it is one of theatre's popular yet, paradoxically, relatively overlooked forms. Monodramas have proven their artistic strengths in professional and amateur productions, yet surprisingly few playwrights think of writing them. The monodrama can be a powerful theatrical work, often using elevated language and powerful images to create poetic enlargement of the character and subject.

Length

The monodrama's playing time can vary from ten minutes to several hours. Short monodramas, highly condensed experiences that make them theatre's equivalent to poetry, often are performed in intimate settings, off- or off-off Broadway, or regional and amateur theatres. You may write a single monodrama or a collection that can be presented individually or as a group, such as Jane Martin's series of eleven short works under the collective title of *Talking With. . . .*

The short monodrama is the smallest theatrical canvas, yet it is a valid artistic form in its own right and can make an exciting theatrical experience for writer, actor, director, and audience. It also will help you improve significant aspects of your playwriting skills such as shaping your play with a beginning, middle, and end; developing rich, dimensional characterization; writing dialogue that is theatrical, concise, and appropriate for the character; expressing your personal vision; and communicating from stage to audience.

Longer monodramas, with playing times equivalent to fulllength plays, have had notable successes on Broadway. Examples of modern full-length monodramas include Jay Presson Allen's *Tru* and Jane Wagner's *The Search for Signs of Intelligent Life in the*

Universe (subsequently made into a movie with Lily Tomlin repeating her stage role).

A number of full-length monodramas are biographical. For example, monodramas have been written about politicians such as Theodore Roosevelt (*Bully!*) and Harry Truman (*Give 'Em Hell, Harry!*), playwrights such as Tennessee Williams (*Confessions of a Nightingale*) and Lillian Hellman (*Lillian*), and poets such as Emily Dickinson (*The Belle of Amherst*), Edna St. Vincent Millay (*A Lovely Light*), and Gertrude Stein (*Gertrude Stein Gertrude Stein Gertrude Stein*). Autobiographical monodramas, though fewer in number, are also popular, illustrated by Spalding Gray's *Swimming to Cambodia*.

Actors write monodramas to create performance opportunities, as did Hal Holbrook, author of *Mark Twain Tonight!*, and Eric Bogosian, who wrote *Drinking in America*. Other monodramas spark actors' careers, such as the *Whoopi Goldberg* monodrama that launched Ms. Goldberg's film successes.

Characteristics of the Monodrama

The monodrama is a flexible form with few apparent rules except the need to entertain in the sense of "enter into," bringing the audience into the world of the character. You capture and hold audience attention with excellent insightful characterization and carefully selected language that is appropriate to the character.

Number of characters. Although only one character is onstage, you can imply the presence of others, usually offstage. One effective playwright's technique is to have the character assume the other characters' personalities and voices: Instead of the character saying "Mother always told me that love is merely biological quests . . ." you might write:

> Mother. Full of advice. (*In the mother's voice, stern, blunt.*) "Chemistry, Jane. Chemistry. That's all there is to love. Hormones, biology, and chemistry. Don't let such foolishness turn your life into chaos." (*Her own voice.*) Yeah, sure, Mom, that takes care of the magic. Some recipe for relationships. Thanks a helluva lot.

Note that the above technique avoids the past tense: The character's mother is, in effect, talking now, so the character doesn't have to say, "Mother told me . . ." Samuel Beckett's *Krapp's Last Tape* uses a variation of that approach: The character listens to tape recordings he made to celebrate each birthday.

Conflict. The theatrical law of conflict doesn't always apply to monodramas; you'll find short monodramas that are effective despite the lack of conflict, depending instead on characterization and word choice. But other monodramas are constructed around a major conflict, a decision the character must make *now*. "What will I do about the way my brother continually abuses me sexually? Telling my parents will destroy them. Is suicide the only way out?"

A fresh insight into the character's world. Monodramas often conclude with a snap, a piercing insight, such as Jane Martin's *French Fries*, which focuses on an old lady whose major goal is to live at a McDonald's because, she says at the end, "You have to have a dream. Our dreams make us what we are." The play makes the audience think about dreams of living at McDonald's and, by extension, our values within society's fast-food life-style.

To Whom Is the Character Speaking?

As you envision your monodrama, you may wonder to whom the person speaks. Why does he or she talk aloud? If possible, simply ignore the question—the character speaks, and that's all there is to it. Still, some playwrights worry about motivation, putting inanimate objects or pets onstage to which the character can speak, but stuffed teddy bears and the like tend to look artificial (and just how many characters would have parrots or goldfish?).

It is better to invent a dynamic character who must speak, is compelled to disclose the inner self, who simply cannot remain silent because of a powerful need to express deeply held beliefs. That approach will help you answer the question, "But to whom does the character speak?" Think of the powerful "Soliloquy" ("My boy Bill") from *Carousel* or "Memories" from *Cats* or "The Story of Jerry and the Dog" from Albee's *The Zoo Story* or "To be or not to be" or any of the other soliloquies that give Shakespeare's characters added dimension.

Some monodramas establish the presence of others onstage, of course invisible and silent. For example, Lanford Wilson's *A Poster of the Cosmos* puts the solo character in a police station's interrogation room, talking to cops who surround him. The playwright wisely avoids having the others "speak," which would cause unfortunate pauses while the character listened and then repeated the information for the audience.

Strengths and Weaknesses of the Monodrama

The monodrama is to theatre as poetry is to literature—short, clean, a direct penetration of the topic. Like excellent poetry, at its best the monodrama is a shining gem, a glittering and rich illumination of an individual's heart and soul, a compelling story that is carefully shaped with a beginning, middle, and end. At its worst, like poor poetry, a monodrama is self-indulgent, wordy because the author fell in love with his or her own voice, too often full of whimpers about failures that are best left hidden in one's diary, and as shapeless as a dirty sock.

THE ONE-ACT PLAY

Like the theatrical monodrama, the one-act play defies rigid definition; you'll find it is a flexible, diverse, often experimental, and intensely theatrical form. The one-act has an honored tradition: We can say that the early Greek playwrights wrote a form of one-acts, although John Millington Synge's *Riders to the Sea* is often considered the formal beginning of the modern form. Many well-known playwrights have written one-acts; some, such as George Bernard Shaw, Eugene O'Neill, Eugène Ionesco, and Edward Albee, started their playwriting careers with one-acts. You'll find excellent one-acts by contemporary playwrights such as Lanford Wilson, Sam Shepard, Joanna Glass, David Mamet, and others. One-acts are popular in high school play festivals or contests, college studio theatres and play direction classes, off- and off-off-Broadway, regional theatre's "second season" productions, and coffeehouses and restaurants.

Length

The one-act, a theatrical version of literature's short story, demands a judicious economy. It varies in playing time from perhaps thirty minutes to over an hour; most are around forty minutes long. The Actors Theatre of Louisville sponsors contests to popularize the "ten-minute play," but so far it has not had widespread acceptance. At the other end of the spectrum, Jean-Paul Sartre's *No Exit* is close to an hour and a half, illustrating the longer one-act form.

Characteristics of the One-Act

A one-act is like a high-speed photograph of the split-second instant that an object drops into a fluid, causing a diadem of droplets to spray up into the air: From that moment you can infer what the fluid was like before the object struck, the force of the object and what it did to the fluid, where the droplets will go, and what the fluid will become later. The unassisted eye never sees that action. So, too, your one-act is an intensely concentrated moment. The "object" is a conflict. The action implies the whole of the characters' lives, a single incident that sums up their past, present, and future. The audience's eye could not have seen the importance in that moment without your play's guidance. Your goal is to find the moment that encapsulates the characters' lives.

One incident. By definition a one-act is a compressed dramatization of a single incident or sequence of action, unlike a full-length play's expanded multiple incidents or actions. Shakespeare's *Macbeth*, for example, has a number of incidents; one of them, such as the banquet scene, could be an effective one-act. The one-act often appears at its best when it condenses the action to a single intense moment that implies a past or future, such as Israel Horovitz's *Hopscotch* (which evokes the two characters' history) and John Olive's *Minnesota Moon* (which implies the two characters' future).

Why now? You can structure your one-act (as well as your monodrama and full-length) more effectively if you know why it must take place *now*. Why does it happen today, not yesterday or tomorrow? What makes this particular moment so important? Answers will give your play a greater sense of dramatic urgency.

Number of characters. The one-act's brevity limits the number of characters, and all must be essential to the play. Too many characters result in thin characterization. Although no one wishes to limit the number of characters—the best rule is "as many as your play demands"—a helpful guideline is to think of two to perhaps four characters. An otherwise excellent playwriting book says you can't write a successful one-act with only two characters, but that is clearly incorrect, illustrated by a number of excellent two-character one-acts such as *The Zoo Story* by Edward Albee and the previously mentioned *Hopscotch* and *Minnesota Moon*. Three characters provide good interplay, as in the eternal triangle. If the initial design for your one-act includes more than, say, three or four characters, consider combining several characters into one. Certainly plan to eliminate utilitarian characters who make no major contribution to the action.

Unification. Effective one-act plays maintain unity of action, focused on one particular conflict; unity of place, within a single physical location; and unity of time, without changes of time. One-acts are so short that a blackout or break in the action, to shift scenery or indicate passage of time, interrupts the flow, disrupts audience focus on the action, and damages the play's unity. If you find you need several scenes, identify the single crucial scene and ask yourself if the entire play can take place there.

The one-act does not like being confined, however, and you find variations in form and content. Some effective one-acts move freely through time and space without interrupting the action, such as *Pvt. Wars* by James McLure and *Canadian Gothic* by Joanna Glass, and a few others call for blackouts to indicate changes in time and space, such as *The Dance and the Railroad* by David Henry Hwang.

Strengths and Weaknesses of the One-Act

The one-act is at its best when sharply focused on a single significant incident, with excellent characterization and a story that is sharply compressed into its essentials. One-acts are carefully edited with a keen sense of theatre to eliminate unnecessary words and action. Freedom to explore new forms often creates exciting theatre. At its worst, the one-act falls victim to its experimental nature, seeking merely to be different (forgetting that originality does not necessarily equal quality) and ignoring commonsense structural elements.

THE FULL-LENGTH PLAY

Is your idea a mural that requires a number of actions or incidents to show the play's theme and conflicts, the development of an involved story, complex character evolution and change, and possibly movement in time and space? If so, you're probably thinking of a full-length play, theatre's largest and most complicated form. Like the novel, the full-length must have contents that demand enlarged size.

Length

The full-length play provides an evening's entertainment, usually two to two and a half hours of playing time. The length is rather arbitrary, not because it is somehow "best" for excellent art but in part dating back to early twentieth-century Broadway productions that attracted suburban commuters who had to catch the last train home. Regardless of the reasons, full-lengths now follow the tradition.

As you would expect, some playwrights defy the conventional length, most notably Eugene O'Neill, whose *Mourning Becomes Electra* and *Strange Interlude* are each five hours long, and David Edgar, whose adaptation of Charles Dickens's novel, *The Life and Adventures of Nicholas Nickleby*, ran eight and one-half hours. Audiences for these long plays arrive at the theatre in the afternoon, leave for dinner at an intermission, then return to see the rest of the play. Those exceptions aside, however, today's full-length plays intend less strenuous entertainment.

Characteristics of the Full-Length Play

Think of your full-length play as a story so rich in detail that it demands full-length treatment. One guideline is to be sure your full-length play simply cannot be told in shorter form. For example, we can't imagine effective short versions of plays such as Charles Fuller's *A Soldier's Play*, Beth Henley's *Crimes of the Heart*, or Lorraine Hansberry's *A Raisin in the Sun*, which all have a scope that demands full-scale expression. Avoid trying to make a full-length by adding scenes ("padding") to what should be a short play, such as Eugène Ionesco's *Rhinoceros*, which has large chunks that easily could be eliminated without damaging the basic idea.

Number of acts. An act is the largest division of your play, consisting of a unified group of activities and containing smaller divisions such as beats, segments, and scenes. Modern full-length plays are two or three acts, with the two-act structure more popular for drama (in contrast to comedy) because one less interruption permits the playwright to make the action more intense. The five-act form, once standard, is out of style; a four-act form never materialized.

Conflict. Your full-length will have one major through-line conflict, typically involving a protagonist fighting to achieve a goal against determined opposition. The conflict starts early at the point of attack, is continually refreshed and refocused with comlications, and finally reaches its peak at the climax. The protagonist succeeds or loses. Secondary conflicts, usually lasting for only a scene or two, are directly related to that single basic struggle. Longer secondary conflicts may be *subplots*.

Incidents. Unlike the one-act, full-length plays have more than a single incident or action. Shakespeare's plays, for example, tend to have some twenty-five or so incidents. No one can state just how many incidents are necessary to sustain the full-length because some playwrights create brief incidents, and therefore will have more in their plays, while others write elongated incidents, requiring fewer to develop the story and hold audience attention. Comedies typically have more incidents than dramas or tragedies.

Most full-length plays also have more characters than one-acts. If necessary to develop your story, full-length plays can change time and place; this is infrequently done during an act but is more often done during the intermission break between acts. Such changes are not essential for a successful play.

Strengths and Weaknesses of the Full-Length Play

Full-length plays are powerful communications that at their best pull the audience into a new world, bringing delight and wonderment. The length allows a broad-sweeping canvas. At their worst, they wander without shape, forgetting that economical statement is as essential as in short plays. Some start with fire but lose strength in the second half because the conflict can't sustain the effort.

THINKING OF AUDIENCES AND TYPES OF THEATRES FOR YOUR PLAY

Regardless of the size of your canvas, your first goal is to write a play that satisfies you. It must be true to itself. In this sense you write for yourself. But being a playwright also requires thinking of your play's "audience," represented by the sort of theatrical organization you hope will produce your play. Think of appealing to that ideal theatre's various strengths, economic conditions, artistic goals, acting and directing skills, and especially its audience, whether young people or adults, in religious or secular settings. That affects such matters as cast size and production values (scenery, lighting, costumes, properties, sound, and so forth). It also may influence your choice of dialogue and action, based on your awareness that some audiences may object to what is euphemistically called "adult language and situation."

What Theatres Present Monodramas and One-Act Plays?

Short plays, such as monodramas and one-acts, typically are presented by small, intimate theatres and workshops, especially in off- and off-off Broadway theatres. The short play is particularly popular in educational theatres: College students present one-acts in studio theatres as part of their directing class assignments, and high schools present one-acts in contests or festivals. Your play will receive earnest and thorough directing and acting in such theatres, but they seldom can afford complicated or expensive production values. Scripts demanding full-scale production values, such as elaborate sets, usually are rejected by such theatres.

Collections of unified one-acts, such as Robert Anderson's *I Never Sang for My Father* and Neil Simon's *Plaza Suite*, have been presented on Broadway, treated as full-length plays. Often the individual units are popular in college studio theatres.

What Theatres Present Full-Length Plays?

Full-length plays are standard fare for Broadway and regional professional theatres, as well as community, dinner, and educational theatres. These productions usually are well financed and are mounted on well-equipped stages. Full-length plays therefore tend to receive lavish sets, scenery, costumes, and lighting. Nonetheless, playwrights writing for Broadway or professional theatres are advised to consider production costs, calling for only one set and relatively few performers. Educational theatres, on the other hand, often search for large-cast plays and are not reluctant to use complex production values.

EXERCISES

Reading

1. Examine a monodrama, one-act, and full-length play. Other than length, what differences do you see? What similarities?
2. Write a brief outline of each of those plays, describing the action. What happened before the play began (the inciting incident)? What sparks the conflict (the point of attack)? What does the protagonist want? What obstacles are in his or her path?

Writing

3. Shape a brief outline of a monodrama you might write. Assume it will be short, perhaps with a playing time of ten minutes. Although monodramas can succeed without conflict, think of a character with a powerful goal that is opposed by an equally powerful force. Describe the character's major emotions. What does he or she want? Why? What obstacles prevent the character from achieving that goal?
4. Build a brief outline of a one-act you might write. Assume you'll have not more than three or four characters and that all action happens in one time and place. Think of a thirty- or forty-minute play. Start the one-act in the middle of ongoing action (*in medias res*), and let background information (exposition) come later when it sparks the action.
5. Construct a brief outline of a full-length play you might write. Be sure all action happens now, not in the past, and drives toward a future. Who is the protagonist? What does he or she want? Why? How strongly? Who opposes his or her goal? List the events in order. Don't worry about act divisions yet; instead, think primarily of each scene of action. To help you better understand the action, try giving each scene a descriptive title that indicates what happens.

A commercial painter paints flat; you can put your finger through. But a painter—for example, an apple by Cézanne has weight. And it has juice, everything, with just three strokes. I tried to give my words just the weight that a stroke of Cézanne's gave to an apple. That is why most of the time I use concrete words. . . . I think what the critics call my "atmosphere" is nothing but the impressionism of the painter adapted to literature.

—Georges Simenon

4

Where Do You Start? Turning Your Ideas into Plays

Writing is the only thing that, when I do it, I don't feel I should be doing something else.

GLORIA STEINEM

When I stop writing, the rest of the day is posthumous. I'm only really alive when I'm writing.

TENNESSEE WILLIAMS

A dedicated writer's lavish expenditure of time and energy could bewilder an efficiency expert. Even your friends and family may wonder what takes you so long to get your play going: Isn't writing merely a matter of putting down your ideas?

Well, no. Seldom is it that simple.

Although outsiders may believe writers start with a complete vision of what they'll create and then simply follow that path, being a playwright is more a process of search, exploration, and discovery. Certainly it is efficient to begin with a clear knowledge of all aspects of your play, but often you must write to find what you want to write, encountering new ideas through writing, confronting what you believe as you write, focusing your thoughts and making choices, always thinking of writing to make your ideas come to life through the alchemy of the theatre.

- A troubled father-son situation may have been the germinal idea for Arthur Miller's *The Price*.
- Actions involving racial conflicts and violence, even murder, provide the germinal situation for Charles Fuller's *A Soldier's Play*.

Starting with Character

If your germinal idea is a fictional, real, or historical person, you're beginning with character. Likely you hear and see selected aspects of the character in your imagination, although you may not yet know the details that surround those glimpses. For illustration, perhaps you're fascinated by the character of Abraham Lincoln. You might wonder, "What was the source of Lincoln's greatness? How did Lincoln cope with what he saw as his countless defeats? What was the essence of his inner strength that helped him overcome depression so he became president?" Your interest is human psychology, the workings of the psyche, a specific human's emotional and intellectual reactions to major difficulties.

Write your ideas about character. As you think about aspects of the character, you'll start getting a number of ideas. Write them. Now you are thinking of the essential qualities; later you'll fill in details. Also write what you hear and see the character saying and doing. At the same time you'll get ideas of what happens (situation) to make the character speak and act, and you'll begin to recognize what the character's actions mean (theme). Write down those insights.

Characters that led to plays. Interest in character starts many plays. Again we can imagine how writers begin their plays, using the following four illustrations.

- Perhaps Shakespeare wondered how two young lovers would deal with violent parental objections, leading him to develop *Romeo and Juliet*.
- Tennessee Williams thought of a desperate woman seeking refuge as he began creating *A Streetcar Named Desire*.
- Peter Shaffer clearly was fascinated by the complex personality traits of Mozart, leading him to write *Amadeus*.
- Neil Simon says that *The Odd Couple* started as he observed his brother Danny's reactions while rooming—and fighting—with another man.

Starting with Theme

If your germinal idea is an issue that grips you, you're starting with a theme. You might believe, for example, that "AIDS is a catastrophic epidemic that strikes down males and females, regardless of national origin, sexual preference, or age. The best remedy is awareness; we have to learn about the disease, who it affects, what an individual can do." Your thoughts are toward the play's subject, ideas important to you, often reflecting contemporary values and problems.

Write your ideas about theme. At this point you seek to identify the issue, examining your beliefs. Write your thematic idea, perhaps starting with a straightforward statement of the issue; later you will look for subtle ways to communicate the material through a play. As you examine the topic you'll find that you're also getting ideas about the people (character) who are living the issue and the events (situation) that awaken their interest and concern. Be sure you write down these ideas.

Themes that led to plays. Modern theatre contains many examples of playwrights' interest in theme.

- Arthur Miller saw thematic parallels between modern political persecution and Puritanical witch-hunts, leading to his drama, *The Crucible.*
- Harvey Fierstein's *Torch Song Trilogy*, a collection of three one-acts, has strong thematic qualities in its examination of homosexuality and family.
- Christopher Durang's thematic concern about an aspect of Catholic teaching led to his *Sister Mary Ignatius Explains It All for You.*
- Jean-Paul Sartre clearly was influenced by thematic interest in the philosophy of existentialism, leading him to start his *No Exit.*

WORKING WITH YOUR GERMINAL IDEAS

A writer's creative ideas are like flashes of lightning bugs on a warm summer evening. They flick on unexpectedly and then move away, temporary glimmers of light that are difficult to catch. Being a playwright requires capturing each insight, whether large or small, so you can use it in your play.

Avoid Judgmental Conclusions About Your Initial Idea

Criticizing your initial idea is a negative habit that will put you in a deadly frozen state, stopping the flow of creative impulses. The glimmer of light disappears. Not every idea will evolve into a play, but avoid jumping to conclusions such as "That's not good enough," "This idea is dumb," or "That won't work." You can't know the value of the idea until you work it over, weigh it, think of its shape, ask what elements you can add or changes you might make, consider options and possibilities.

Even when you can't immediately find a place for the idea, preserve it carefully so it can germinate. Your subconscious can work on it and you, like many other playwrights, may find later that you suddenly have a vision for a play. That flash of insight isn't sudden, of course; it started months earlier when you had an idea that you saved in your writer's notebook, and your subconscious mind was working it over for a long time before you became aware that the idea had grown and evolved.

Avoid a Quest for "Originality"

Deliberately trying to be original is as dangerous as making judgmental conclusions about ideas for plays. A quest for originality is a false priority that will make you dismiss otherwise valid concepts, and the more you try to be somehow novel or different, the more likely your play will be trendy but lack genuine substance. Avoid artificial evaluative standards about your ideas such as "This isn't different enough," "Oh, no, that's been done before," or "But this won't prove to others that I've got a really creative mind." Your personal input into that germinal seed, your insertion of *self*, is the true mark of originality.

Record Germinal Ideas in Your Writer's Notebook

Regardless of the size or detail of your original idea, discipline yourself to capture it immediately by writing it in your writer's notebook, preserving it for future use. Saying, "Oh, sure, I'll remember it" leads to loss of ideas: You'll forget more than you retain. More significant, the act of writing enhances ideas and creates fresh insights, and you'll discover that writing all ideas that come to you will encourage your subconscious to continue feeding ideas to you.

Being a playwright means writing; recording your ideas in your notebook is an excellent step toward that goal. Fragments of dialogue, interesting characters, puzzling situations, intriguing stories in newspapers or magazines—all of these and more will give you glimmers of ideas for plays and therefore belong in your writer's notebook.

Keep your writer's notebook with you at all times to record ideas the moment they occur. You'll find you're building a rich treasure chest of creative impulses, thoughts, and ideas about situation, character, and theme. These will help you with the play you're now writing and give you materials for future works.

FLESHING OUT GERMINAL IDEAS

Any category of germinal idea—situation, theme, or character— can start your writing process; any one of the three can lead you to write a compelling play. Of course these are the beginning steps. Ahead of you is further search to identify what you will write, and then you must transform the idea into a work for the stage. A two-step creative and imaginative enhancement process will amplify that first seed, then add more depth.

First Two Steps to Enhance Your Germinal Idea

Focus the idea. Whether you start with situation, character, or theme, first you amplify your original idea. Put it in sharp focus. Mull it over. Make it specific, lively, vital. Examine it in detail, adding dimension, giving it flesh, investing yourself in the idea, looking at it from a number of views to enlarge and enrich the seed. Make choices. Ask yourself questions—we'll discuss some below—to cultivate the seed and create a strong plant.

Add details about the other two categories. You don't want to write a play based narrowly on only one of the three categories, so while you enrich your first idea, you refocus your creative sensitivity on the other two categories. For example, if you start with a germinal idea for character, flesh out your vision of the character, then repeatedly ask yourself questions to help you see the theme and situation that are major influences on the character's existence. Equally, if your first idea has to do with situation, seek details about theme and character. If you begin with theme, consciously work to add rich character and situation. Your goal is to be sure all three categories are equally strong forces in your play.

Example of Amplification Process

Imagine you are deeply concerned about a specific theme having to do with marital problems. That's too broad, so you narrow the focus. Assume your interest has to do more specifically with a husband's demeaning attitude toward his wife. Amplify that theme. What is your personal involvement in the theme? Why is it important to you? Define your ideas. Precisely what is a "demeaning view"? Start thinking about the idea as a stage piece: What actions *show* the husband's attitude?

Examine the characters. You already know two characters are necessary—husband and wife—so start with them. What does each have at stake? What does each want? What goal is each pursuing? Why does the husband ignore her worth as a human? What causes him to view her negatively? Perhaps you'll conclude that he does love her, but his attitudes are based on false values. What attitudes? Why does he have them? Are his false values products of society or environment? How? Why? Shift your attention to the wife. What are her reactions to the husband's actions? Why did she marry him in the first place? Does she love him? What actions show her feelings; what does she do? Did she help create the problem? How?

Consider other characters. You can write the play about only the husband and wife—there are a number of successful two-character plays—but additional characters often increase tension and help you show action that otherwise might have to be told. Who else might be involved in the action? Do you need friends or other family members? If so, how are they directly involved? What does each want? What goals? Start identifying other characters, being sure they are essential to the action (instead of convenient for the playwright). Describe them. What are their emotions?

Find the situation. Probably you'll set the play in their home. Describe it. You'll need a conflict, something that sparks the action, forcing it to happen now (instead of yesterday or tomorrow). What is the crisis? What caused it? What happens? What are the actions? What are the physical or psychological events, predicaments, and emergencies?

Translate Issues into Actions that Show the Idea

You could write an essay telling readers your conclusions about marital problems, but plays *show*. Tell yourself that your play can never state the problem directly—a good guideline is to assume the characters do not know the thematic issue or problem and therefore can't speak it clearly—so you search for actions.

How does a playwright develop all three categories? You undoubtedly know numerous illustrations, but here we can cite one. In 1879, Ibsen used the theme-to-situation-to-character process to write his drama, *A Doll's House*. Boldly ahead of his time, he examined particular marital problems. We see how the playwright shows the basic problem in the following scene that begins the play. Asterisks (* * * *) indicate omitted material. Nora has just entered the living room, loaded with packages.

HELMER: (*From his study.*) Is that my little lark twittering out there?

NORA: (*Busily undoing the packages.*) Yes, it is.

HELMER: Is that my little squirrel bustling about?

NORA: Yes.

HELMER: When did my squirrel get home?

NORA: Just this minute. (*She puts the bag of macaroons back in her pocket and wipes her mouth.*) Oh, Torvald, do come in here! You must see what I have bought.

HELMER: No, don't disturb me! (*A moment afterward he opens the door and looks in—pen in hand.*) Did you say "bought"? That— all *that*? Has my little spendthrift been flinging money about again?

*   *   *

HELMER: Nora! (*Goes to her and pulls her ear playfully.*) There goes my little featherbrain!

*   *   *

HELMER: (*Following her.*) Come, come; the little lark mustn't droop her wings. Don't tell me my little squirrel is sulking!

Ibsen *shows* Helmer's attitude toward Nora, his little squirrel, featherbrain, and lark. No doubt the man loves her, but he sees her neither as a human nor as an adult woman. The playwright could have chosen to tell the audience—for example, he might have included a narrator saying the play will deal with a wife's need to be free, or a scene with Nora and a confidante in which the latter tells Nora to reject Helmer's treatment, and the like— but that would have drastically reduced the play's impact. Note, too, the playwright's use of foreshadowing: Helmer is worried about money, which will become a major complication in the play. Ibsen combines theme, situation, and characters in a powerful drama.

THE "MAGIC IF" STIMULATES CREATIVITY

The "magic if" can increase the creative development of your ger- minal idea. If you have acting experience, you know a variation of the system, recommended by Russian acting mentor Konstantin Stanislavsky, which requires asking a series of "what if" questions. An actor cast as Macbeth, for instance, develops his character by asking "What if I were alive centuries ago: What would I feel and do if I suddenly encountered the apparently supernatural 'weird sisters' who promised I would become king?" Note that the ques- tion doesn't encourage the actor to think what *he* would do in those circumstances; instead, it puts him into the character's world.

Playwrights use similar creative "what if" questions to develop theme, situation, and character. For example, you might ask your- self, "What if two former friends happen to meet accidentally after years of separation?" Enrich the situation with other questions: "What if each is a 'success' in one reference but nonetheless hates his or her life? What if they *discover* (a vital part of theatrical characterization) significant insight into themselves and each other?" Add to your idea by examining the situation and char- acters. What happens? Who are they? What does each expect from the other? What will they do?

Such "what if" questions gave Lanford Wilson his poignant play, *The Great Nebula in Orion.* The two characters are former college friends who meet by accident. Both appear highly successful, one as a New York dress designer and the other as a wife. Yet as the play progresses, each discovers that the other suffers from emotional losses. That discovery leads each to see she leads a hollow life.

Asking "what if" kinds of questions can stimulate your imagination by a form of role-playing, putting yourself in the situation. "What if I meet someone from my past with whom I had shared an important relationship? What if one of us wants to restore what we had, but the other cannot? What if we both want to go back to the past? What if we don't recognize how much we've changed?"

Asking such questions stimulates your creativity, prompts your subconscious to think of solutions, and helps you see more deeply into the characters and possible alternative ways of bringing them to life. Avoid censoring the questions or rejecting them because they appear of little value to your play; instead, let one question lead to another in a form of freewheeling brainstorming. While some questions may be of little direct value, all can be important because they help you create additional questions and ideas.

DO YOUR IDEAS HAVE THEATRICAL POTENTIAL?

If I didn't know the ending of a story, I wouldn't begin. I always write my last lines, my last paragraph, my last pages first, and then I go back and work toward it. I know where I'm going. I know what my goal is. And how I get there is God's grace.

—Katherine Anne Porter

I think the theatre should try to be emotional, colorful. I think everybody's tired of stages where nothing happens. The theatre is the art of the emotions—it is also that of the concrete.

—Boris Pasternak

How can you be certain your ideas will be theatrical? Which ideas are best suited for a play? There's no guarantee you'll know until you actually start writing, but certain guidelines can help you test your idea to see if it is stageworthy. Later chapters will amplify these concepts.

Is the Idea Based on a Major Conflict?

Drama requires force against force, a battle for survival, whether physical, psychic, or psychological. Does your germinal idea have a major conflict? Is the conflict a result of the central character's basic desire? Can you see a way of sustaining the conflict throughout your play? Do you envision the conflict being *shown* instead of being *told*? Is the conflict important to you?

Do You Know Whose Play It Is?

Do you have a clear idea of the central character? Does the play focus on that one person? Will he or she start the action and remain active throughout the play? Do you know the strong goal that the central character will pursue during the play? Is that character strongly motivated to want that goal? What does the character have at stake—what will be lost if he or she doesn't get that goal? Is the character emotionally involved in the action? Do you like the character? Will the audience be sympathetic to the character?

Are the Characters in Opposition?

It is easier to construct your play if you create characters with strong motivational needs and goals that make them oppose each other. Do you know all major players in the action? Do you know their emotions, hopes, dreams, relationships? A major portion of your play's structure is based on characters in conflict, people whose nature and beliefs make them react to each other with clashes, strong will against opposing strong will, powerful desire thwarted by contrary will. Do they have something at stake, an emotional investment in the outcome? Think of Romeo and Juliet opposed by their families, Othello opposed by Iago, Amanda opposed by Tom. Oppositions create conflict, helping you see what happens in your play. Are the characters dimensional? Do you have a clear view of their complex personalities? Do the characters have playable emotions that actors can bring to life?

Do You Have a Way of Structuring the Idea?

Think of the situation or "what happens" in your play. Do you know the order of the conflicts? Does the conflict and action build? Are conflicts based on the characters' oppositions? Just as you describe a play to a friend who didn't see it—"this happened and then that happened"—situation is the shape and design of the activity or "what happens" in your play. It is based on your decisions about what your play will *do* (in the sense of the Greek word *dran*, meaning to do, from which we derive *drama*). Do you see a series of dynamic happenings?

Can You Show the Action?

The Greek word *theatre* meant a seeing place, and you write so audiences can see the play's action evolving and in motion as they watch. You select and design events that are important to show the audience your vision, helping them see, feel, and hear the action, creating an experience that changes the audience from passive viewers to active participants. Think of "a doing of action." Do you see a series of linked dramatic actions, struggles between the forces, entrances and exits, incidents and scenes, complications, discoveries, and major events? The action and arrangement of the conflicts between the characters most often involve the protagonist's drive to achieve a goal; and you show the changes and evolutions of characters as they react to obstacles and each other.

Do You Know When the Action Begins?

Plays take place in the present tense, moving to a future. Therefore they are uncomfortable when they contain too many references to the past. Do you know the specific moment to begin your play so it flows inexorably from the present toward its future? Do you know why the action must happen *now*? Do you see a sense of immediacy and urgency in the action?

Do You Know What Happens in the Play's Middle?

What are the events, the happenings? Are there enough to sustain the action? Can you sustain the conflict over the course of the play? The amount of conflict may dictate the size of your canvas. Does the germinal idea lend itself to showing? Unlike the novel, a play doesn't tell the audience the implications of the action or what the characters are thinking. Can you see and hear the events and characters?

Do You Know How the Action Ends?

Not all writers echo Katherine Anne Porter's statement that she must write the ending before the beginning of her story—some writers say they start at the beginning without knowing where things will go—but her system makes sense because it gives her a target at which she aims as she writes. Do you know how your play ends? If not the specific conclusion, do you know the mood, upbeat or down, happy or sad?

EXERCISES

Take your time working through these exercises. File your notes in appropriate locations in your writer's notebook.

1. Write a situation you would like to turn into a play. First describe the situation in one or two paragraphs. Then add details. What makes you interested in the situation? What starts the action? Why? What happens? What are the major incidents? What causes them to build in intensity? How does the action end? Put the events into a logical order.

   When you've completed this step, describe the characters who would be involved.

   Then specify what the action would mean to an audience watching it.

2. Write about the central character you'd like to have in a play. Describe the character in detail, using two or three pages. Why does this character interest you? What does he or she want? What are the character's major emotions?

   After you've finished identifying the character, write details about situations that would show aspects of the character you think are most significant. What other characters would be necessary to bring that character to life?

   Then write the conclusions you'd like audiences to reach after seeing this character brought to life.

3. Write about a theme that is important to you and that you'd like to make the core of a play. Describe it in two or three pages. Why does it interest you? What makes it important? Define what the theme means to you.

   After you've finished describing the theme, write details about the people who would live the theme, showing it by their lives and actions.

   Describe the situation in which the characters would live.

4. Of the three germinal ideas above, which is most important to you? Amplify the idea in detail. Translate the idea into actions that show what you want audiences to see and feel.

In creating, the only hard thing's to begin;
A grass blade's no easier to make than an oak.
                                        —James Russell Lowell

A writer needs three things, experience, observation, and imagination, any two of which, at times any one of which, can supply the lack of the others.
                                        —William Faulkner

5

Creating Characters: People in Action to Achieve Their Goals

*I deliberately look for colorful people. They're very right for thea-
tre. Theatre has to be theatrical. If you can get color into the
accountant, you've got something. Write the whole thing first
and then say he's an accountant. That's a very wacky accountant, but so what? Theatricality feeds and challenges the actor,
the director, and the designers.*

—LANFORD WILSON

Character or plot—which one should you think of first when you
start to plan your play? Which is more important to make a good
play?

Aware that playwriting is an art that attracts creative writers
with firm convictions, you won't be surprised to discover that
questions involving the supremacy of character versus plot will
produce two diametrically opposed beliefs held by equally fervent
supporters. One suspects that a poll of playwrights would reveal
a fifty-fifty schism of opinions about the relative importance of
character or plot.

Some playwrights say emphatically that the structure of action
is the most important element in a play—audiences are interested
in what happens in a play—and therefore you should focus on

plotting your play before considering character. After all, the plot unifies your play.

Others, just as emphatic, say that character is more important than plot—audiences are interested in the people of a play—and you should first establish your play's characters before considering its structure. After all, characters unify your play.

Clearly, given the wide differences of opinion, neither extreme is correct. Or both are. Although for the purposes of discussion here we necessarily must discuss character and plot separately, in fact they are two halves of a whole, and an accurate description of the importance of these two elements can be stated simply: Plot is character in action.

Characters and plot work together. Characters are the soul, spirit, flesh, and blood who give shape to your play, and plot is the skeleton and muscles that hold the play together. Characters have basic superobjectives that create conflict and twists and turns that form plot, and plot provides complications and stimuli that force characters to react and change. Neither plot nor character exists independently of the other; each contributes to the development of its partner. Being a playwright means developing character and plot equally so each enriches the other.

Whether you believe plot or character is more important in writing for the theatre, one premise is inescapable: *Plays that involve characters in conflict are more effective than plays that do not.* As August Strindberg says, playwriting requires "seeking out the points where the great battles take place." Dramatic intensity, comic or tragic, is a product of characters willing to battle to achieve something highly important to them and who have something highly important at stake that gives them a personal involvement in the struggle and outcome. "Great battles" make characters dimensional and interesting. The battles also make them easier, even fun, to write because their intense concerns are so active that they often dictate what they want to do, sometimes making the playwright think the characters are writing the play themselves.

Exercises you completed in previous chapters have started your identification of characters you'd like to create, and your writer's notebook should be full of ideas and materials you can use to develop your play. Here we look at using those notes to create theatrical characters.

WRITING CHARACTERS TO ATTRACT PRODUCERS, DIRECTORS, AND ACTORS

Being a playwright requires constructing theatrical characters who will attract the attention of producers and directors and make them want to present your play; give actors artistic challenges with playable emotions and actions to help them bring characters to life as you intend; and communicate to the audience so they can understand and appreciate characters, action, and theme, sustaining interest in your play. Dynamic, colorful, contrasting, active, and clear characters serve your needs.

Actions Show Characters

Producers, directors, and actors look for characters who are shown primarily by actions, although other clues are helpful (like other characters' descriptions or stage directions), and therefore you write dimensional characters who are a direct result of the number of incidents that stimulate characters to act. Think of your characters—most especially the major ones—progressing, evolving, unfolding, in motivated steps. You want to think in present tense, building characters who are thinking "I am doing" instead of "I did," and are aware of their future, thinking "I want to achieve" an important goal.

Clues to Character

Directors, actors, and audiences expect to learn about characters through certain clues you give them. Among the primary clues are the following:

- What the character does; action
- What the character will not do; action through inaction
- What the character says
- What the character does not say; communication through silence
- The character's emotional range
- What the character wants; goals
- Why the character acts, speaks, or seeks a goal; motivation
- How the character responds to stimuli
- Self-descriptions
- Descriptions by others

• Stage directions, descriptions
• The play's environment

Throughout this chapter we'll examine how you use these clues.

THE PLAYWRIGHT AS ACTOR: USING THE ACTOR'S APPROACHES TO CHARACTERIZATION

Outstanding performers such as Laurence Olivier, Dustin Hoffman, Glenn Close, and Meryl Streep have developed techniques that result in excellent characterization. You can borrow their methods, such as those suggested below, to write dimensional characters for the theatre. Writing with actors in mind has two distinct advantages: It helps you write interesting, stageworthy characters, and it makes actors more interested in performing in your play.

Two Basic Acting Techniques

Actors use two different approaches to bring character to life, an "outside-in" technique that starts with externals such as age, dress, physical mannerisms, and vocal qualities; or an "inside-out" method that first looks for motives, environmental and hereditary influences, memories, and psychological drives. Either approach—or the more typical combination of both approaches—leads to dimensional characterization. Keeping those acting techniques in mind, you can construct characters to challenge actors.

External Qualities

The actor's outside-in technique starts with the character's given conditions. Through stage directions, action, and dialogue you can identify qualities such as the following:

Age. Age influences behavior—a teenager reacts to certain stimuli differently from the way an older person does—and therefore you can use it to indicate characters' special qualities, experience, and view of the world. For example, the youth of the boy and girl in Benjamin Bradford's *Where Are You Going, Hollis Jay?* creates a comic and poignant situation because this is their first experience with love and they haven't learned how to speak about their emotions. Equally, the advanced age of the man and woman in D. L.

Coburn's *The Gin Game* creates the forlorn, lonely situation of two people in a nursing home, both with such set ways of thinking and behaving that they are in constant conflict.

Physical mannerisms. Characters may pose or posture to indicate certain behavior mannerisms such as pomposity, courage, or the like. In Anton Chekhov's *The Cherry Orchard*, for example, one character continually pretends to play billiards; in Bernard Pomerance's *The Elephant Man* the character distorts his body to represent physiological deformities that shape his thoughts. Use such mannerisms judiciously to depict character traits.

Vocal mannerisms. Some characters may speak hesitantly and others speak quickly and authoritatively. You can describe such mannerisms in stage directions, but dialogue and actions are more important tools. For example, in *The Caretaker*, Harold Pinter uses dialogue to show a character's internal turmoil: "But . . . but . . . look . . . listen . . . listen here . . . I mean. . . . What am I going to do? (*Pause*) What shall I do? (*Pause*) Where am I to go?" Such techniques, although effective for characterization, are used carefully so the play won't become languishingly slow.

Overall appearance. Is the character neat? Messy? Proud or indifferent about appearance? Why? How does that exterior appearance reveal the inner person? Directors, actors, and costume designers will take the playwright's statements, plus the character's clues, to create a special visual quality that depicts the character. You use stage directions to help those artists "see" each character; more important, you guide them by the character's behavior and actions.

Names. Although you don't want to use old-fashioned epithets (Mrs. Straightlaced, Mr. Pinchpenny), characters' names often suggest personality qualities. Listen to the differences in names such as Brucie versus Biff, Cecily and Iris, or Jimmy-Bob and Simon. Note that you want names to have distinctly different sounds; similar names may confuse the audience.

Characters Are Part of the Play's Environment

Directors, designers, and actors study the basic given environment of the play that you define through stage directions (as well as action). Equally, you'll better understand your characters and the play's situation by considering a number of environmental influences. Some are suggested below.

Time environment. Characters often react to and are part of the time in which the action takes place (year, season, hour of day or night, progression of time).

Physical environment. Characters are influenced by their locale, such as the visible setting in which the play takes place (a room or bus station, for example), the outside environment (small town, metropolitan area, and so forth), and the particular region (southern, western, for example).

Educational environment. The educational level(s) of the characters, as a group or individuals, contributes to who they are. Are your characters college-trained? Did they fail to graduate from high school? Does that educational background influence how they feel about themselves and what they say and do? The primary characters in Eugene O'Neill's *The Hairy Ape* have little or no educational background, which influences their speech and actions; in contrast, characters in Edward Albee's *Who's Afraid of Virginia Woolf?* are well-read, literate college graduates, as shown in their dialogue and actions.

Economic environment. Wealthy, poor, or middle class, the economic status of the characters can dictate their attitudes and actions. Characters in William Saroyan's *The Cave Dwellers* and Lanford Wilson's *Hot L Baltimore*—the hotel is in such disrepair that the "e" has dropped out of the name—have distinctly limited financial resources that dictate their responses to the forthcoming eviction from their homes.

Social environment. Characters belong to a general social world and are influenced by their status. The social environment of Oscar Wilde's *The Importance of Being Earnest* dictates a great deal about the characters, in contrast to that shown in O'Neill's *The Iceman Cometh*.

Political environment. Characters form a particular structure within the play—the pecking order, so to speak—and also may be involved in a larger political issue (abortion, AIDS, minority rights, and so forth).

Religious environment. Characters are influenced by an implied or explicit presence or absence of a deity-structured universe. Classical Greek plays such as Sophocles' *Oedipus Rex* show humans with direct relationships to their gods; some modern plays such as Samuel Beckett's *Waiting for Godot* take place in an environment that does not have religious guidance.

Action

The actor's inside-out technique includes a search for the character's actions. It requires finding a single active present-tense verb to describe his or her overall movement throughout the play, and comparable verbs for the character's actions in all speeches. This method involves thinking of "what I (the character) am doing" in the play, and the actor looks for actions that reflect the internal aspects of the character. For smaller units, such as speeches or scenes, actors think of active verbs that motivate the character: "I plead," "I beg," "I ignore," and so forth.

You can use a similar approach to give your characters a consistent driving-forward movement. Keep focused on the characters' motivations and desires, what they do caused by what they want, and how they respond to other characters' actions. In your mind as you write is each character's needs, wants, and goals. You think: At this point "A" wants to get "B" to do a favor; now "B" refuses "A" by changing the subject; "A" pleads; "B" ignores the request; "A" demands; "B" decides to make fun of the request as a way of refusing it; and so forth.

Biography

The inside-out acting technique requires actors to create involved biographies to discover the internal truth of the characters they portray. They ask literally dozens of questions about the character, a few of which we indicate here:

> Where was I born? Who were my parents? What were their occupations? What were my largest successes in high school? Failures? Who was my first love? Why? What did I do while in love? How did I handle the loss of that love? How did I react to various rites of passage such as adolescence, first sexual experience, reaching the age of majority, marriage, first child, divorce, death of a relative, and so forth? What did I dream I'd do with my life? How do I feel now about those dreams?

Through continued questions, the actor begins to understand the character. Many actors actually write their character's biography (with insightful conclusions that often surprise, even shock or delight, the playwright who created the character).

A similar approach will help you know your characters more fully. Writing each character's life story will give you answers to such questions, which in turn will give you new insight into the characters, resulting in richer and more dimensional characterization.

Descriptions by Other Characters

You can create a need for others to describe the character. Banquo defines Macbeth's character, Tom describes Amanda and Laura (who describe him), Blanche describes Stanley (who describes her), and the opening scene of Edmond Rostand's *Cyrano de Bergerac* contains a number of secondary characters who describe Cyrano's remarkable nose, swordsmanship, and heroic qualities.

Character's Self-Definition

You also can find reason for the character to explain his or her personal traits. Self-definitions or descriptions often are vital ingredients of soliloquies such as "To be or not to be . . ." but modern theatre, which avoids such devices, uses dialogue between characters. For example, note the instant clarity in the opening lines of Anton Chekhov's *The Seagull*:

MEDVEDENKO: Why do you always wear black?
MASHA: I am in mourning for my life. I'm unhappy.

Lanford Wilson's *Ludlow Fair* uses interesting self-definition when a character looks sadly in the mirror at herself and says self-deprecatingly that little can be expected from a person named Agnes except a large bosom and a propensity for chest colds.

SOURCES FOR THEATRICAL CHARACTERS

I think it's true of most playwrights that their characters—male and female, young and old—are just aspects of themselves. When I people the stage with all these souls, what I do is split myself up. I implode and all these little fragments tear around inside me like crazy and become the characters.
—Tina Howe

The Writer's Eye

According to playwright Mario Fratti, theatre "is a window open on the lives of our fellow creatures." Being a playwright requires a special desire to open windows that allow you to see the people around you, carefully observing humans in action, noting how they show attitudes and emotions. Look around. The reclusive woman on the corner who is the subject of neighborhood rumors, the recently divorced man with a new flaming red sports car, the latchkey teenager who is known as a troublemaker, the church elder recently convicted of purchasing kiddie porn, the medical doctor who changed careers and now teaches third grade—your writer's eye observes these and other people in your world, and your imagination works to understand them.

With your writer's eye you spy into other humans, giving you insight that leads you to write characters who show their feelings. Some writers say that their "eye" is disturbingly active even during highly emotional personal experiences such as funerals, marriages, family breakups, and childbirth. One portion of the writer is deeply involved in the situation, but another portion is observing the other participants, recording them for future writing. The spying doesn't always please friends or family members: James Thurber said his wife often came to him at parties and demanded, "Thurber, stop writing!" A writer's eye notes tensions, emotions, motivations, and concrete actions, not abstract descriptions; a playwright's eye into theatrical characters starts with giving them actions and emotions that lead them to change and evolve.

Ideas for characters come from various sources, and perhaps you'll be one of the fortunate playwrights with a large flow of possibilities for plays. If the well appears dry, however, don't despair and—most important—don't stop writing. You can stimulate your creative energy by exploring your world for new ideas. We can indicate some major sources below.

Yourself

Tina Howe, author of *Painting Churches*, says that a basic source for characters is the playwright's self. Many writers agree. Much of what you write is necessarily autobiographical, and it is wise to allow yourself freedom to let your plays reflect portions of your beliefs, attitudes, ethical and religious standards, memories, dreams fulfilled or lost, family relationships, frustrations, loves, angers, and other aspects of your inner self.

"Every character I imagine is part of me," says playwright Maria Irene Fornes. You don't have to be a murderer to write a character who is a killer, but you do reach into recesses of your inner self to find emotions that might lead to killing someone, and you examine your memories for times that you took violent actions which your imagination enlarges and expands to help you get into the nature of the particular killer you need for your play. As Fornes says about using herself to create characters, "The sadistic captain in *The Conduct of Life* and the victim of that sadistic captain— you can't *write* them unless you *are* them. If a character is brutal, it is because I am brutal. I take the blame and the credit. No writer can write a character unless she understands it thoroughly inside herself."

You might decide to make your play directly and recognizably autobiographical, focused on significant incidents from your past or present. Some playwrights find that their most meaningful events involve their families because such relationships are filled with powerful emotions that deeply influence the writer. Personal familial experience can lead to excellent autobiographical dramas or comedies, evidenced by plays such as Eugene O'Neill's *Long Day's Journey into Night*, Tennessee Williams's *The Glass Menagerie*, and Neil Simon's trilogy, *Brighton Beach Memoirs*, *Biloxi Blues*, and *Broadway Bound*.

Alternatively, you may want to create a less recognizable, indirect reflection of yourself or a metaphor for an important aspect of your life. Playwright David Hwang says, "I'm quite aware of the extent to which my own life is embedded in the things I write. I'd like to think it's not obvious to the casual observer. Essentially, what I do is take the essence of the experience and transmute it into a form where the specifics are different. Take *Dance and the Railroad*. I've never worked on a railroad, but I have understood what it is like to be at war with yourself over your own artistic impulses, in the battle between commerce and art." That indirect, metaphorical approach can be highly successful, as indicated by plays such as Arthur Miller's *The Crucible* and *After the Fall*.

You may, if you wish, disguise autobiographical qualities to the point that not even your closest friends or relatives will recognize your presence in the play. You're the fountainhead of the character's origin, but the play, like a broad river, then takes its own course. Expect the artistic needs of the play to require reshaping or changing events, situations, and characters. Such changes probably will further disguise the actual incidents, but nevertheless the play captures the essences of the experience.

Friends and Relatives

Next to yourself, you are most familiar with friends, relatives, and associates. Your close knowledge of them can help you draw dimensional characters in your play. Study those people you know best, seeking to understand their actions, emotions, motives, beliefs, driving forces, ethical standards, dreams, ambitions, and reasons for behavior. You'll discover aspects of character that can help you write your play.

Imagine, for example, that your play requires a protagonist who is liked and respected by others in the play, and you want the audience to have similar reactions. To help you create that protagonist, select a close friend you and others respect and carefully study his or her character, paying special attention to actions. Look beyond mere surface qualities, such as appearance or clothing, and ask what your friend does that results in positive responses from others. What are the essential behavioral patterns and qualities that make a person liked? What creates respect? Select specific instances when your friend took particular actions that show those qualities, then adapt those actions for use by your protagonist. Comparable observed behaviors, positive or negative, can become part of other characters.

You can draw from friends or relatives to find ideas for plays as well as characters. Neil Simon says he wrote a play (which later became a movie and television series) about his brother Danny. "I saw the story being lived out," Simon says. He suggested that his brother write it himself: "What's going on between you and Roy Gerber—it's a play. Two guys living alone, and the two of you are fighting like husband and wife. You've got to write it as a play." Danny did write about fifteen pages but was unable to see how to complete it, so Neil wrote it: *The Odd Couple.*

News Media Stories

Local, national, and international events provide excellent ideas for plays, and the news media are filled with materials you may shape into a comedy or tragedy. Look for stories that deal with personalities, problems, politics, and the like. News accounts, however, tend to treat stories in an abstract, dispassionate tone, requiring you to invent a more personalized, often smaller scale that involves specific humans. For example, a news story about a famine striking an entire country might become a play if you envision a character attempting to overcome problems delivering food to a small village, perhaps in conflict with an indifferent, greedy bureaucrat who cares more for personal gain than for the starving people. Other stories may be more complete, needing only your imaginative shaping and personal point of view. For instance, news accounts about a date rape or an AIDS victim may be ready to build into a play because they already have protagonist, antagonist, and plot.

The Imaginative Composite

Theatrical characters most often are composites, one trait from a friend, a second personality quality from a relative, attitudes or experiences from your own past, and so forth. Your imagination blends the pieces into one character, and as Lillian Hellman notes, the character's independence and the artistic needs of the play will dictate further changes.

> *I don't think characters turn out the way you think they are going to turn out. They don't always go your way. If I wanted to start writing about you, by page ten I probably wouldn't be. I don't think you start with a person. I think you start with the parts of many people. Drama has to do with conflict in people, with denials.*
> —Lillian Hellman

NECESSARY CHARACTERS FOR YOUR PLAY

Identifying the essential people for your play's action is your first priority in planning the play's list of characters. In one of playwriting's paradoxes (and if you're thinking theatre is constructed with paradoxes, I quite agree with you), you think of the characters in two different ways, as independent humans yet also as pawns who serve the play.

Theatrical Characters Have Independent Lives

On one hand, you want to see each character as a unique human with strong emotions, desires, traits, and mannerisms. Creating a dimensional character requires knowledge of his or her background, parents, friends, education, occupation, and dozens of other details. In this sense you want to create characters with independent lives aside from the play.

Theatrical Characters Serve the Play

On the other hand, although each character is independent, each must also serve your play, filling specific functions in the overall scheme of the play. In this sense, each is an important tactical chess piece you use to develop your play's strategy. Think of characters as contributors to the theatre's logic and needs; create characters who will take the actions that your play's structure and development require. The two major characters that serve your play and provide the central conflict are the protagonist and the antagonist.

THE PROTAGONIST

The word *protagonist* has several sources. *Pro* means for, and *agon* means struggle or act, and therefore the protagonist is a character who struggles for a goal, acting to achieve something. The term also comes to us from the Greek word that meant first combatant, an excellent description of your play's major character because the protagonist's struggles are the source of dramatic action.

In *effective plays there is one dominant force: A central character has a deep desire, even a compulsion, to achieve something, seeking that superobjective despite all opposition—other characters, interior personal doubts, environmental or hereditary influences, even fate or the gods—until he or she wins or loses.*

Drama consists of a protagonist with a goal, a combatant eager to win a particular victory, matched against equally strong opposition. Granted, it may be possible to write a successful play without a protagonist, but it is hard to imagine why a playwright would want to omit the protagonist given the many advantages the character contributes to your play's conflict, tensions, character interplays, meaning, organization, and plot. Why would some playwrights avoid the protagonist? Perhaps they feel that the protagonist-antagonist structure is just old hat, and they are driven by a need to be original at any price. Or they may think that protagonist is the same thing as flawless hero (it isn't), and they want to write about humans with flaws and dimensions (which are quite appropriate for a protagonist). Some writers, one fears, simply don't know how to create a protagonist. None of these reasons appear sufficiently strong. Whether exemplary hero or, more typically, a lesser mortal with human weaknesses but still trying to achieve something, the protagonist keeps your play in focus by engaging the audience's interest and emotions, giving them a connecting point through whose eyes they view the action.

The Protagonist's Contributions to Your Play

Have you attended a confusing play and wondered, "But whose play is it?" The answer should be "The protagonist's," if the playwright has a clear vision of characters and story. The protagonist is your play's central character; his or her powerful, active need to achieve a goal will give your play action, life, power, and unity. The protagonist's drive for a goal also helps you organize the play's structure or plot. For example, the plot movements in *The Glass Menagerie* are a direct result of Amanda's overpowering need to give Laura a secure future—in Amanda's terms, that means a husband—and the play's action, characterization, and diction are logical outgrowths of the protagonist's objective.

The Protagonist Awakens
Audience Interest and Emotions

The protagonist propels your play forward, initiating and receiving action, creating audience interest in the outcome. Because the protagonist has something vitally important at stake and therefore is emotionally involved in the action, he or she awakens the audience's emotional reactions and gives them someone for whom they can care. Usually, although not always, the protagonist's values echo the audience's sensibilities—he or she is the good guy, so to speak, who seeks a goal the audience approves—but most often you'll want to create a more complex character with additional qualities, perhaps weaknesses, or with vulnerable holes in an otherwise apparently secure control. Amanda's goal, for instance, is praiseworthy, but some of her personal traits show human weaknesses, and audiences will at times sympathize with Tom when he simply can't take any more of his mother's pressures and pretensions.

The Protagonist Shows the Play's Meaning

The audience perceives your play's thematic core through the protagonist's struggles and actions to achieve his or her goal. For example, through Macbeth's increasingly desperate actions to gain more power, the audience understands the play's basic meaning about power's ability to corrupt. In *Death of a Salesman*, Willy Loman's struggles to make his son love him illustrate the playwright's thematic concept about disasters that occur when moral values are badly warped.

The Protagonist's Goal

Must the protagonist have a goal? Yes. One definition of a protagonist is "a character actively striving to achieve a particular goal." The protagonist's goal may be meticulously planned or haphazard, conscious or subconscious.

Must the goal be stated? Not necessarily. You'll find the protagonist's goal stated explicitly in some plays, such as *Hamlet*, Sam Shepard's *Fool for Love*, and Samuel Beckett's *Waiting for Godot*. The goal is implied by the protagonist's actions in other plays, such as *Macbeth*, Henrik Ibsen's *A Doll's House*, and Arthur Miller's *Death of a Salesman*.

Must you know the protagonist's goal? Absolutely. Otherwise the character will wander aimlessly, and the play's structure will be haphazard.

Why create a protagonist with a major goal? The protagonist's goal helps you write your play by giving your plot a central struggle. It also is important for actors and directors involved with bringing your play to life. Consider these advantages the protagonist gives you while writing your play:

- The protagonist's goal unifies your play. As the protagonist pursues that goal, he or she both initiates and receives action—the action centers around him and his movement toward that objective—and the protagonist's constant drive to achieve a goal gives the play its forward motion.

- You create the plot's "complications" (discussed in the next chapter) by creating obstacles in the path of the protagonist's goal.
- A vital and dynamic protagonist's goal gives your play a better chance of production because directors often look for a determined protagonist.
- Actors are trained to look for the "character's superobjective," and they develop characterization according to what they perceive as the character's "through line of action." Both phrases refer to what the playwright calls the goal. The stronger you make the character's objectives, the better the possibility you'll be satisfied with the actors' interpretation and performance of your characters. But if goals aren't clear in the play, the actors' creative urges will insert characters' objectives, important changes that quite possibly will change your characters, even your play, in ways that will distress you.

The Protagonist's Plan

The protagonist's goal produces a master plan of action that begins at your play's *point of attack*, or the beginning of the action, discussed in the next chapter. The plan may be implied through the situation or explicitly stated, such as Hamlet's speech, "The play's the thing wherein I'll catch the conscience of the king." The protagonist may have to devise additional or secondary goals to overcome obstacles, but the master goal always dictates his or her actions and sustains the play's action until the climax. The goal also helps you construct your play's action, consisting of steps the protagonist will follow.

Using the Protagonist's Goal in Your First Plays

Create a protagonist who desperately needs to achieve a goal. You should know it, even if he or she is too inarticulate to state the objective, or too confused to recognize it. Your writing process will be easier if you continually ask questions such as: "What does my protagonist want? Why? What stops him or her from getting it? How does the protagonist respond to each of those obstacles? What emotions drive him or her to pursue that goal?" Answers will help you shape the play's conflict while also developing the play's characters. Write the goal and plan on a piece of paper, tack it to a bulletin board above your keyboard, and refer to it often as you construct your play.

THE ANTAGONIST

Drama is conflict, the arrangement of force versus counterforce, conscious will to achieve a goal against equally determined opposing will, one individual (the protagonist) against at least one and sometimes several adversaries (the antagonist). Hamlet must achieve his goal—to avenge his father—and is opposed by his mother and uncle. Lear has every reason to want to achieve his goal—to keep the trappings but not the responsibilities of being a king—and is thwarted by two of his daughters and their husbands.

The Antagonist Contributes to the Play's Action

If there were no force-counterforce, there'd be no conflict and therefore neither drama nor action; without an antagonist, the protagonist would simply achieve his or her goal, and the play would quickly end. In contrast, an antagonist helps you sustain your play's structure of action: Each step the protagonist takes to achieve his or her goal is opposed by the antagonist, creating complications that maintain the plot. The antagonist can be a single, powerfully compelling character like Iago, or might be a number of characters like those who oppose Cyrano de Bergerac.

The Antagonist Must Be a Worthy Opponent

We measure our fellow humans by the size of the obstacles they encounter and the manner in which they struggle against adversaries, admiring those who tackle fearsome odds. There's little honor in bashing a weak opponent. For many of us the final outcome is less interesting than the struggle: Responses to opponents, win or lose, are fascinating because those struggles give us insight into the person. So, too, your protagonist's character is tested and shown by reactions to the antagonist, such as Proctor's struggles against the forces of wickedly blind intolerance in *The Crucible*. A strong antagonist gives you opportunity to develop the protagonist's character and helps you structure and sustain the play's action.

The Antagonist Makes the Characters More Dimensional

The importance of the antagonist as a counterforce is illustrated by Lear, who changes and evokes audience emotional responses only because of the actions of his two daughters: If those counterforces did not exist, Lear would never need to change. Without an antagonist your play would have little character evolution; with one, the protagonist has reasons to react, change, and evolve as a result of new stimuli the antagonist provides.

The Antagonist Within the Protagonist

Interior doubts. Hamlet doubts his ability to find a proper course of action and often is indecisive; Macbeth is crabbed and confined by fears; Amanda Wingfield's unreal expectations stop her from finding a path to help Laura; Willy Loman doesn't recognize his values are so wrong; and John Proctor is so guilt-burdened over his affair with Abigail that he is ambivalent about taking action to correct moral mistakes in his society. In these sorts of plays the protagonist must battle a strong inside opposing force, an interior antagonist that both gives the character dimension and contributes tension and conflict to the play.

Exterior representation of inner doubts. Yet while we recognize the dramatic value of such interior conflicts and admire the resulting fascinating characterization, we must guard against a conclusion that they will suffice. A character battling his or her own self is intriguing, but exterior forces—the antagonist character—are necessary to show the interior battle and provide visible and playable conflict. Hamlet, for example, is opposed not only by himself but also by a number of antagonists, most notably Gertrude and Claudius, and his interior struggles are not enough to provide conflict and tension to carry the play forward.

By all means, think of your protagonist's interior battles, doubts, and insecurities as you plan your play, but think also of exterior representation of those struggles. That will lead you to develop one or more characters who show the play's conflict. You show the opposing force best with antagonists who share the field of combat with the protagonist.

SECONDARY CHARACTERS SERVE THE PLAY

It is possible to write an effective two-character one-act or, less frequently, full-length play, focused on protagonist against antagonist, but additional characters can add fire and dimension. A two-character play can grow static, while additional characters add conflict and interest. More important, other characters make your writing process easier by providing necessary stimuli to force protagonist and antagonist into further action.

Characters have independent lives... The paradox we mentioned earlier—characters as people versus characters as servants of your play—also applies to secondary characters. Like the protagonist and antagonist, they must have independent life and a significant role to play in the development of both the protagonist and the play's action. In this sense you write characters who are distinct individuals, not types.

...but characters also are masks of dramatic action. On the other hand, secondary characters also serve your play's structure and growth by emphasizing the conflict, adding tension to the situation. Although Richard Schechner refers to directors and actors, his point is equally pertinent for playwrights when he speaks about characters serving the play: "Great errors are made because performers and directors [we would add playwrights] think of characters as people rather than as *dramatis personae*: masks of dramatic action. A role conforms to the logic of theatre, not the logic of any other life system. To think of a role as a person is like picnicking on a landscape painting." In this sense you write characters who fall into theatrical categories to serve structural needs.

Examples of Secondary Characters "Serving the Play"

What do we mean by characters "serving the play"? How do you use them? Because the entrance of a new character usually is a complication, you use secondary characters to spark the plot by judiciously planning when they enter the scene, perhaps bringing in a new character when the play begins to drag due to lack of new insights or flagging conflicts; and because they can be drawn to contrast with the major characters, you shape them to point up the special traits of protagonist and antagonist. Use them, too, to add texture, color, differences, and other qualities to enhance your play.

The poker players in *Streetcar* illustrate a playwright's use of secondary characters to make major contributions to the play's primary characters and structure. Although the players are not dimensional humans and one might argue that they should be eliminated because they are not essential to the play, they are important in a number of ways:

- The game shows Stanley's macho character as he plays poker with "the boys."
- During the game Stanley is crude and authoritative, even dictatorial, giving the playwright another way of showing that Stanley is king of his castle.
- The poker players amplify Stanley's character. If Williams had written the play with only Stanley visible, audiences might conclude that all males in that universe are dictatorial. But putting other males in contrast to Stanley reinforces his particular values and behaviors. The scene shows that Stanley is not like other males in the universe of this play.
- The scene allows Williams another opportunity to use different techniques to show aspects of Blanche's character as she displays herself seductively, standing in bra and thin slip with the light behind her, yet carefully making her actions appear accidental. The action shows the character clearly: She uses sex to get attention while pretending to be the quintessential "lady." It reinforces Stanley's complaint that Blanche is pretentious and hypocritical, and it contributes to Stanley's motivation to rape her ("We've had this date with each other from the beginning!" he says, referring to her displays of her body).
- The poker game serves to introduce Mitch and Blanche. Although Williams could have invented another device to put the two together, this approach helps show Mitch's immediate fascination with her: He stays with her instead of returning to the poker game, even after Stanley shouts for him to return.
- The scene serves as a change of pace. Much of the play prior to this scene had been constructed with duets and trios involving Stanley, Stella, and Blanche; the poker game brings other people into the play, making a refreshing change.

Color and Texture

Secondary characters can serve your play by adding a grand sweep, color, and texture. Viewed strictly, Edmond Rostand's heroic verse play, *Cyrano de Bergerac*, actually needs only the three parties involved with the love story: Cyrano, Roxane, and Christian. But the play's sweeping size and poetry require equally powerful visual effects, and the secondary characters, although many are one-dimensional, make major contributions to the overall effect. So, too, Peter Weiss's *The Persecution and Assassination of Jean-Paul Marat as Performed by the Inmates of the Asylum of Charenton Under the Direction of the Marquis de Sade* (more commonly known as *Marat/Sade*) requires a large number of secondary characters to create the background of feverish insanity so important to the play.

The Subject

The protagonist wants something, perhaps another person or an abstraction such as freedom or revenge. Either will be best represented by a concrete character. For example, one character may want love and security, but those qualities are personified by another person: For Romeo there must be a Juliet, for Macbeth there must be a Duncan, for Willy Loman there must be a Biff. Equally, Hamlet may want justice or revenge, both abstractions, but more concretely he seeks to ascertain the guilt of Claudius and Gertrude. As you construct your play, think of a character who can serve as the subject for your protagonist's needs.

The Visible Objective

Amanda's objective—a husband for Laura—influences the structure of *Glass Menagerie*. Williams could have written the play with references to various possible suitors, describing Laura's various encounters with them, but that would have decreased the play's emphasis on present and future. Amanda's objective almost forces the playwright to bring the suitor onstage, leading to the creation of the Gentleman Caller, visibly showing Amanda's objective. So, too, Mitch is a visible objective in *Streetcar*, showing Blanche's need for someone to take care of her. Without Mitch the play would not show the growth of Blanche's hopes and her subsequent despair. You may be able to develop your play with a character who will turn an abstract objective into human reality.

The Pivotal Character

Some playwriting books say the protagonist is the play's pivotal character, but this more properly refers to the character whose opinions, important to the play's process, influence the audience's responses to the protagonist's goal and the basic conflict. To some degree the pivotal character is similar to the *raisonneur*—voice of reason—who appears in older plays to express the author's point of view.

You use the pivotal character to bring the audience to new insights because they are likely to echo the pivotal character's search for truth, changing opinions with the character. Such characters may be in an authoritative position, perhaps judging actions or characters, like Reverend Hale in *The Crucible*, a significant pivotal character who first seems to believe in the powers of witchcraft but then changes his opinions radically during the trial—"I denounce this trial!" he shouts—because he discovers that hysteria and prejudice, not reason or religion, are ruling the court. His discovery helps the audience see that justice is lost in blind conformity.

The Close Friend

In *The Crucible*, Proctor has his wife; in *Hedda Gabler*, Hedda has Mrs. Elvsted; in *Cyrano de Bergerac*, Cyrano has Le Bret; in *Death of a Salesman*, Willy Loman has Ben; in *The Time of Your Life*, Joe has Tom—all protagonists who have close friends, confidant(e)s with whom the protagonist can share inner thoughts, plans, or doubts that otherwise would have to be expressed in a soliloquy, an outdated technique which of course you want to avoid because it tells instead of shows. If you find that your protagonist needs opportunities to express personal secrets, consider building a close friend into your play.

CREATING THEATRICAL CHARACTERS

Just before I started working on Hot L Baltimore, *I read Dickens's* Our Mutual Friend. *I had just done* Lemon Sky *and* Serenading Louie, *and they seemed pale and quaint*

*compared to Dickens. I knew I had to goose my work. I knew
I had to have characters that were more far-out. Your characters have to have some magic.*

—Lanford Wilson

Wilson took his own advice, finding "magic" not only for characters in his *Hot L Baltimore* but for his many other plays, including *Fifth of July* and *Burn This*, making him an acknowledged
master of characterization. If that's the result of "goosing" characters and making them "more far-out," he proves that his advice
works.

Effective theatrical characters are vivid, unusual, and different,
yet they must also be plausible, possible, and probable within the
basic concept of the play. Dimensional characters are like onions,
constructed of layers of traits that are slowly disclosed to the
audience, with surprises which nonetheless are still an inherent
part of the onion's core.

Creating characters for your play is a process similar to the
novelist's, with some important differences: Theatrical characters
must be playable, which means you write for actors to show
thoughts and emotions. And they must have a basic instant clarity
so the audience can recognize their driving force. Theatrical characters are perhaps more colorful, which you achieve by creating
dimensional qualities for individual characters and contrasting
them against a range of characters with different qualities.

The Tip of the Iceberg

Dimensional and interesting characters are structured like ice-
bergs: Although only one-tenth shows above the surface, they are
supported by a foundation that is nine-tenths of the whole. The
better you know your characters, the stronger they will be and the
more new ideas you'll find about their personality and actions.
You'll discover interesting traits, emotions, and drives by ex-
panding your view past the actual play, paying special attention
to aspects that will not show in the play. Construct lengthy notes
about the characters' lives before and after their lives onstage
(Where were they before they entered? Where will they go when
they leave?) and before and after the specific action of the play.

Emotions

Theatre is the art of emotions; emotional action is the play's life
force. Emotions give your characters a rich vitality, making the

play snap and crackle. Try to give each character a primary energetic emotion—happiness, sadness, anger—connected to his or her basic goal. Major characters should also have emotional ranges and motivated changes—such as happiness interrupted by sadness and anger, laughter mixed with tears, and the like—although you may decide that a single emotion is adequate for secondary characters. Blanche, for example, goes through a wide range of emotions; Mitch has only two (love for Blanche, followed by anger that she lied to him); the poker players have one at most.

Audience empathic responses. Characters' emotions are important communications with audiences. As you think of your reactions to plays you've seen, you quite likely will remember your own emotional reactions to the characters' happiness or tears. Empathy, the audience's psychological identification with characters, is an engendered response that causes the audience to be drawn into the play, pull for the hero to win or the villain to be thwarted, wish the best for the young lovers, cry with their loss.

Identify which characters you want the audience to empathize with, then give those characters vivid emotions the audience can recognize and feel. You may wish to write emotions that show a softly vulnerable character like Laura's in *Menagerie*, a desperate hunger like Blanche's in *Streetcar*, a driving discontent like Pale's in *Burn This*, or other recognizable qualities. Emotions must be sustained, believable, and plausible—rapid or unmotivated emotional change smacks of soap opera writing—which means they are motivated by situations and other characters.

Theatrical Characters Are Constructed with Opposite Qualities

Planning your play involves finding contrasting characters who will serve the play's needs because they are in opposition—strong, unbending oak and slender, giving willow, bright sun against dark night, uncertain Hamlet and decisive Laertes, corrupt Macbeth and unswerving Banquo, gentle, loving Cordelia and selfish, cold Goneril and Regan, failed Willy and successful Ben. Opposition is not enough, of course: The characters must have reason for their differences, and you must also think of a basic harmony of differences so all characters, despite their contrasts, belong in the same play.

Unique Fingerprints, Not "Typical"

Just as each human has unique fingerprints and DNA charts, so each of your characters has his or her distinctive individuality. Avoid stereotypes or thinking of "typical" characters. Instead create characters who have a variety of qualities that make them unlike any other person.

Start with One Basic Characteristic

To maintain focus and clarity of purpose, try starting your creative process by identifying a single dominant characteristic for each of the people in your play. You'll keep your characters moving toward the play's goal by avoiding the temptation of using numerous qualities. Although you want dimensional humans with more than one trait, effective characterization starts with making choices, selecting the one major trait or attribute that drives the character. For example, the three fascinating characters in Jean-Paul Sartre's *No Exit* are based on quickly perceived attributes: the coward, the lesbian, and the nymphomaniac.

Starting with single qualities is not as simplistic as it might sound. First, each character's major quality doesn't show up by itself but instead contributes to the whole picture just as various individual colors in a painting will create a totality. Second, your knowledge of dominant qualities will help you keep the characters consistent and dynamic within their basic parameters. Third, clarity of qualities will help directors and actors bring your play to life as you intend, but if the characters are murky, the actors may perform their roles differently from the way you wish.

After you've clearly identified each character's distinctive attribute, build on that foundation by adding other personality elements. For example, the coward wants to be alone and pretends to be an intellectual, the lesbian enjoys being cruel and is more intelligent and manipulative than the others, the nymphomaniac desperately needs attention and acts various roles to please others, and so forth.

Heightened Life

One way to think of the characters is as real people, and we've discussed using yourself or your friends as sources for your play. However, this does not mean that theatrical characters are real people. Your characters are instead a form of heightened reality, selectively enlarged to show their special traits and desires. Drama is not life but an artistically selected representation of life; equally, theatrical characters are heightened representations of real people. In life, an individual's crisis may evolve over a long period of time, with the person slowly reacting emotionally to the growing situation; in theatre, you think of condensing the crisis, selecting the specific moments that simultaneously show the most significant aspects of the problem and the facets of the character.

Contrast

Contrasted characters give your play dynamic movement, vitality, and interest, and contrast sets each character off from the others and provides a basis for conflict. If you want to write a protagonist who has, say, moral strength, you can emphasize that quality by creating one who is morally weak. For illustration, think of dynamically contrasting characters such as Medea and Jason in Euripides' *Medea*, Macbeth and Banquo in Shakespeare's *Macbeth*, Blanche and Stanley in *Streetcar*, Reverend Parris and Reverend Hale in *The Crucible*, or Eddie and May in Sam Shepard's *Fool for Love*. In *The Crucible*, Proctor's intense desire to do what is fair and just is emphasized by other characters who are cruelly self-serving.

The Colorful and Unconventional

The wacky character, as Lanford Wilson says, is perfect for the theatre. The delightful eccentric enlivens plays, whether the central character or a less important one. For example, in William Saroyan's *The Time of Your Life* a character enters, points to a large letter *W* on his sweater, and announces proudly that it doesn't stand for a jerky high school somewhere but instead refers to him: My name is Willy. Lanford Wilson's *Hot L Baltimore* is peopled with wacky characters who make the play come to life, and Babe, the central character in Beth Henley's *Crimes of the Heart*, is interestingly unconventional (she's the one who shot her husband and then made a pitcher of lemonade).

DECIDING HOW MANY CHARACTERS YOU NEED IN YOUR PLAY

In the above discussions we indicated ways you can freely use characters to amplify and enrich your play. Now we must balance that freedom by introducing pragmatic concerns about the number of characters you use.

Essential and Nonessential Characters

A concept of parsimony influences most aspects of theatre, paring superfluous qualities down to their most economical statement, and affecting such diverse elements as scenery and acting. It applies to characters as well. Essential characters contribute to the play's conflict and help establish or reinforce the protagonist-antagonist struggles. Nonessential characters do not further the action or develop the major characters. Even though they may be convenient for the playwright—servants to answer the phone or delivery people to bring messages or the like—if they are nonessential, you should consider eliminating them from the play.

The Playwright's Juggling Ability

The more characters the playwright puts in the play, the greater the risk that he or she will be like the clown who tries to balance an increasing number of spinning plates on slender sticks, desperately running back and forth to stop one from falling while trying to add another. The clown can handle four or six plates, but after eight or so the chances of plates crashing increase. So, too, the playwright faces problems juggling a large number of characters: It's all too easy to drop a character, to forget that he or she is onstage. For these reasons it is wise to limit your play's cast size to the number you can comfortably handle and keep alive so they make vital contributions to the action.

Characters Are Expenses

Consider the market for your play. If you are aiming at a professional production, be aware that producers look at characters as dollar signs. Because each character is an actor who must be paid and costumed, some professional producers are necessarily wary of the costs of large-cast plays (say, more than eight to twelve characters).

Opportunities for Actors

In contrast to the professional theatre's concern about expenses, most college and high school theatres, which do not pay actors, often look for large-cast shows to increase participation opportunities for student actors. Such theatres expect that all, or at least most, characters will be richly written to challenge actors.

Small Roles

Konstantin Stanislavsky, the Russian acting teacher, once said there are no such things as small parts, only small actors. It sounds like a nice idea, perhaps valuable in building morale of those cast in walk-ons, and is often quoted by directors trying to encourage actors to concentrate on playing the one-line roles. It is also nonsense. Actors who have played spear-carriers or members of the crowd know these are small parts, thankless and uninspiring. If you have small roles in your play, ask yourself if you'd like to be cast in them.

With some clever rewriting you can add details to the character of, say, a delivery person—from a one-line bit ("Anyone here order an anchovy pizza?") to a more interesting and dimensional character. Think of Goldie Hawn playing the role. Or Chevy Chase. Or Dustin Hoffman. Could the scene be enhanced with the dimensionality that such performers would add? Might it make an interesting complication? How would the other characters respond?

EXERCISES

1. Write a detailed character biography of your play's protagonist, using the guidelines suggested in this chapter and adding other information you think is important. Assign the protagonist personal traits that you find worthy of respect, qualities you like in people: You want the audience to care intensely about the protagonist's needs. Be sure the protagonist is different from all other characters in the play.

2. Describe the protagonist's goal—what he or she wants—and why that goal is vitally important to the character. What makes the protagonist want that goal? What will the audience see happening to stimulate the protagonist into action? What does the protagonist have at stake? What is his or her emo-

tional involvement? What is the protagonist doing to achieve the goal? How does the protagonist reach out to involve the audience?

3. Specify the protagonist's single basic characteristic. What are his or her secondary characteristics?
4. Identify the protagonist's emotional ranges.
5. What are the play's environments? How do they affect the protagonist? How do they influence all other characters?
6. Construct a character biography of your play's antagonist, using the guidelines suggested earlier in this chapter. Be certain the antagonist is different from the protagonist, perhaps even directly opposite in selected significant areas.
7. Describe the antagonist's goal—what he or she wants—and why that goal is important. Why does the antagonist oppose the protagonist? What does the antagonist have at stake?
8. Specify the antagonist's single basic characteristic and secondary qualities.
9. Define the antagonist's emotional ranges.
10. Will your play have a "subject"? If so, describe that character in detail.
11. Does your play need a "visible objective"? Describe the character.
12. Will you use a "pivotal character"? If so, describe the character.
13. Would a "close friend" help you establish the protagonist? If so, describe the character.
14. Assign each smaller character distinctly different qualities. Think of polar opposites to build contrast.

I'm convinced that there are absolutely unbreakable rules in the theatre, and that it doesn't matter how good you are, you can't break them. . . . You must state the issue at the beginning of the play. The audience must know what is at stake; they must know when they will be able to go home: "This is a story of a little boy who lost his marbles." They must know, when the little boy either gets his marbles back or finds something better than his marbles, or kills himself because he can't live without his marbles, that the play will end and they can applaud and go home. He can't not care about the marbles.

*He has to want them with such a passion that you are in-
terested, that you connect to that passion. The theatre is all
about wanting things that you can or can't have or you do
or do not get. Now, the boy himself has to be likable. It has
to matter to you whether he gets his marbles or not.*

—Marsha Norman

6

Building Plot: Shaping Your Play's Action

On balance, I feel I did crafted work in my first piece [Five Finger Exercise]. It said what I wanted it to say, and it possessed a shape which made it play easily and finally accumulated its power. This quality of shape it very important to me. I have always entertained the profoundest respect for art, meaning "artefact," and for the suffix "wright" in the word playwright. I hope [my plays] are wrought properly and that they proclaim this fact sufficiently to give audiences a deep satisfaction in their form and their finish. I also hope that these qualities are not too assertively evident—because if a play irritates by seeming to be too well made, this surely means that it has not been well made enough: that smoothness of the joinery is sealing the work off from the viewer.

PETER SHAFFER

A caveat is appropriate before we begin discussing the structure of plot: What follows may strike you as a mechanical, perhaps even arbitrary, approach to playwriting. It is, and it isn't. Granted, plot is complicated with cogs and gears and wheels within wheels, operating like a well-oiled piece of machinery to move the play in its inexorable build to the future. The following discussion of plot's elements will necessarily focus on each piece, perhaps adding to the suspicion that we're looking at a mechanical process.

Construction techniques aside, however, there's no suggestion here that effective playwriting must follow any particular approach, and certainly you never want machinery to show. What follows is a model, not a prescription, for your play; although we look at individual ingredients, we remember that in a well-written play those elements blend and overlap. A playwright's study of technique is matched by an awareness that playwriting art consists of hiding technique.

THREE BASIC DIVISIONS OF PLOT

Plot is the master design of the play's conflicts, the selection and arrangement of incidents to achieve maximum impact, and an organized development of the story in a way that fits your play's particular demands. Plot keeps the play moving forward with clashes that create dramatic tension. Its presence makes a compelling story that enriches characterization, shows the play's theme in action, and creates suspense and mystery to grip the audience's attention; its absence makes a static universe in which nothing happens or changes.

Plot can be subdivided into three basic parts. Part One is introductory material, which establishes the play's initial sense of equilibrium and contains such storytelling devices as exposition and foreshadowing. Part Two is the play's action, which starts with the point of attack that breaks the equilibrium. The second part contains the protagonist's goal, discovery, complications and reversals, and the like, and continues up to the play's climax. Part Three is the ending, following the climax, containing resolution, denouement, and catharsis, restoring a sense of balance in the play's universe. These three parts roughly correspond to the beginning, middle, and end, artistically welding a play into a unified whole. The function of each part indicates relative length and what you want each to accomplish.

Length of Each Part

The beginning, middle, and end are equally important, but they are not equally long. At the risk of being arbitrary, we can indicate general lengths for each part, understanding that your particular play may demand a different form.

Full-length play. Assuming a full-length play around 110 manuscript pages, the beginning is relatively brief, perhaps 5 to 15 pages. The middle contains the major action of the play and therefore is the longest, around 85 to 100 pages. The ending is rather short, around 5 to 10 pages.

One-act play. The one-act typically has proportionally shorter beginning and ending portions. For a 40-page script, the beginning might be 1 to 3 pages, the middle approximately 33 to 38 pages, and the ending around 1 to 4 pages.

These lengths are approximations and must not be followed slavishly, but they do suggest the relative development and importance of each part. Note the brevity of the beginning, indicating that a play should get to the action as soon as possible.

Orderly Sequence of the Plot's Elements

The following discussion looks at a model of plot, discussing each element in the order it typically occurs. Not all plays follow this model, but a careful study of dramatic literature will show you that a surprisingly large percentage of plays—even those considered nontraditional or experimental—use this basic sequence of elements.

PART ONE: BEGINNING— INTRODUCTORY MATERIALS

> *We live in what is, but we find a thousand ways not to face it. Great theatre strengthens our faculty to face it.*
> —Thornton Wilder

The first section of your play introduces the audience to the characters, the situation, and the environment. It includes hints or warnings of forthcoming events. These introductory materials, although important to bring the audience into the play's particular universe, should be relatively brief because they do not contain action.

Design your play's beginning by deciding at what point events must be shown. Three criteria help you select the appropriate moment for your play to begin:

• No earlier portions of the story are necessary for the play's action to develop.

- No additional events are necessary to start the action.
- Start close to the action, even in the middle of ongoing action, to get preliminaries out of the way relatively quickly so you can move to the more active part of your play.

Development of action in time. Think of your story in a time-line continuum from the first moment to the final event. To visualize your story, try drawing a long line on a sheet of paper. Let the line represent time. Mark all incidents that make up the past, present, and future of your characters in chronological order, from beginning to end.

To find the moment that best begins your play, look for the incident on that line which will spark the action and start a series of complications that leads to the climax. For example, Tennessee Williams could have selected any number of points along the line to begin *A Streetcar Named Desire*: Blanche trying to hold Belle Reve together, Blanche dealing with a death at Belle Reve, Blanche with the traveling salesmen at the Hotel Flamingo in Laurel, or even Blanche already at the Kowalski home and having lived there for several months. Any of those points would have told the basic story, but only one beginning meets the three criteria above: The play's beginning starts moments before Blanche arrives at the Kowalskis' because the plot's conflict begins with the initial encounter between Stanley and Blanche. All earlier events, although important, are not necessary for the play's action.

Inciting Incident

The inciting incident is a major event that happened before your play began. Typically the characters do not yet know the full significance of that action, but relatively soon after the play begins they will discover the relevance of that event to their lives. In *Hamlet*, for example, the inciting incident is the combination of the death of Hamlet's father and his mother's remarriage to Claudius; Hamlet discovers the importance of that incident when the Ghost appears. The inciting incident will be linked to the point of attack and told to the audience with exposition.

What's the advantage of the inciting incident? A strong inciting incident gets your play off to a richly dramatic start and eases your writing process. It will strengthen the point of attack and the protagonist's motivation to drive for a goal, which in turn will help you see subsequent action with complications and reversals. Not unimportantly, the inciting incident helps you keep a clear focus on your play's design and gives directors significant insight into your plot.

How many inciting incidents are possible in a play? One. If you perceive more, you'll want to combine them into a single effect on the protagonist.

Can I write a play without an inciting incident? Some experts believe that the inciting incident directly causes the point of attack. Others feel that the point of attack is a cause in itself and therefore can exist without causal factors like an inciting incident. Both sides agree, however, that a playwright can more readily craft a stageworthy plot by using a strong inciting incident to spark the plot.

Must I be sure that the inciting incident is clear? Most playwrights would answer, "Yes, at least in the author's mind." A study of plays will show you that the inciting incident is usually quite clear to the audience. On the other hand, playwrights such as Harold Pinter seem to communicate satisfactorily without a specific inciting incident, using instead vaguely implied conditions. Full-length plays typically are based on a major inciting incident, although some one-act plays and short monodramas appear to lack one.

Exposition

Exposition gives the audience background information regarding the situation, characters, relationships, time and place of the action, and the like. Because it introduces the audience to the play, it traditionally is found in the opening moments. You'll find blatantly obvious exposition in older plays, sometimes delivered by a narrator or a pair of servants. Approximately the first third of Euripides' *Medea*, for example, is heavily laden with exposition delivered by the Nurse, the Chorus, and the Attendant. Some more recent plays have equally conspicuous exposition, using artificial devices such as messages from the radio, television, or telephone. Few directors appreciate scripts with such obvious exposition, and your play has a better chance of being accepted if you develop techniques to hide or disguise exposition.

What's the most effective way to use exposition? Craft exposition so it is subtle; exposition is best when not recognized. Avoid forcing characters to speak or listen to information about facts they already know but which the playwright wants to communicate to the audience. Engage the audience's imagination; implied exposition can be more effective than explicit statements.

Do I use exposition only in the beginning of my play? A full-length play may require exposition at the beginning of the second and third acts to explain the passage of time or other events. Further, you can craft your play so it quickly gets to the action, placing exposition as needed throughout the rest of the play.

How can I hide exposition? Characters should have strong motivation to speak lines containing exposition, which will disguise the technique; avoid servants talking about events in the house, the classic blatant device of delivering exposition to the audience. You can hide exposition materials by placing them in the middle of a speech or sentence, which is the least dominant location; avoid putting them in the beginning or at the end, which are most dominant. Exposition is less noticeable if you give only small bits at a time, instead of large chunks.

How can I use exposition to propel the action forward? Henrik Ibsen's *Ghosts* shows that exposition can be more than a mere recitation of past events. Instead of using one large, heavy-handed glob of exposition, as in *Medea*, Ibsen subtly uses bits of exposition to disclose the past, small pieces at a time, during the course of the play, to motivate the characters. Each new discovery of the past changes the characters, moving the play forward.

Should I use a narrator for exposition? Once popular in classic plays as an introductory device, the narrator is out of fashion in modern theatre and is disliked by directors and play agents. For example, an editor at Samuel French, Inc., a large play publisher and playwrights' agency, gives this blunt advice to playwrights: Never consider writing "narrator" in a script. Too often the narrator is simply an all-too-easy way for the playwright to communicate information to the audience, resulting in a play that tells rather than shows. Notable exceptions come to mind, such as Tom in *The Glass Menagerie* and the Stage Manager in *Our Town*, but one easily imagines that hundreds of plays have disappeared or were never produced because the narrator was an intrusive device.

Foreshadowing

"Something wicked this way comes," say the witches in *Macbeth*, illustrating foreshadowing that focuses audience attention on coming events. Foreshadowing is a classic storyteller's device that creates suspense by warning the audience to expect certain events such as a conflict, crisis, complication, entrance of a major character, or an emergency. It also warns of more general effects and signals the play's basic intellectual thrust, as in the first scene of *Macbeth*, where the witches' chant, "Fair is foul, and foul is fair," foreshadows a world that will turn upside down.

Foreshadowing also helps you write. Each piece of foreshadowing is, in effect, a promise you make to yourself to develop plot, focusing your attention on maintaining action. You can test this idea by planning to include, say, three pieces of foreshadowing in the first several pages of your play, and then designing when and how that foreshadowing will take root and grow during the play.

Do I use foreshadowing only in the opening of my play? No. It can be effective throughout the play, often preparing for a major character's entrance. One does not expect to find it after the climax when action is completed.

Can I write a play without foreshadowing? Probably. But you'll find it so helpful that you'll want to use it, remembering that, like exposition, foreshadowing is best when subtle. The thunderstorm effect, for example, has become such a cliché in drawing-room melodramas that a modern audience may find it comic instead of ominous.

Plant

A companion to foreshadowing, a plant refers to a physical object that will be important later. If a letter, gun, or the like is significant in the last scene, you can have a character find it by accident at that useful moment, but the convenient coincidence sharply strains credibility. Alternatively, you can *plant* the item by having a character discover it in an early scene, make an idle reference to it, and return it to its location. For example, a character may be looking in drawers for a stamp, happen across the important letter, wonder casually about it, put it back in the drawer, find the stamp, and continue. That plants the letter; its later use will not be a contrived coincidence. (Anton Chekhov's advice about plants bears repeating here: "If a gun is hanging on the wall in the first act, it must fire in the last.")

General Mood Setting

Beginning playwrights often write a lengthy introduction designed to set the play's mood and environment. Cut those pages ruthlessly. Mood setting seldom is essential and frequently stops the action. If you are genuinely convinced you need to set a mood, make the passages as brief as possible.

Plays should have a basic mood, but you don't have to devote pages to establishing the mood in the introduction. Instead of working to establish a mood, focus your attention on getting to the play's action as soon as you can. Most often the action will set the mood more effectively than long introductory passages.

A Sense of Equilibrium

Plays start with a certain balance. Forces may be aligned equally, or they might be uncomfortably unbalanced but nevertheless at rest. *Hamlet* and *Death of a Salesman*, for example, begin with a skewed balance—things are not right in the play's world—but nonetheless there is a static balance. The balance will be thrown askew at the play's point of attack, and the rest of the play will show a series of dynamic changes in the balance.

Establishing the correct sense of equilibrium is relatively easy if you have a firm idea of the effect of the point of attack, which throws things sharply out of balance. Often you check your opening's balance after you finish your play and are considering revisions.

"Traditional" Structure Opening a Play

The "traditional model" that guides the structure of a play's beginning includes seven elements of plot: inciting incident, exposition, foreshadowing, equilibrium, point of attack, major dramatic question, and protagonist's goal. We can examine that structure in *The Shock of Recognition*, a comedy by Robert Anderson. Jack Barnstable, a playwright, wants to convince Herb Miller, a producer, to stage his play the way he wrote it—with the entrance of a naked man.

Shock of Recognition begins with fourteen necessary introductory short speeches between Herb and Jack, helping the audience become familiar with characters, their jobs, and the situation. The introduction is compressed—those speeches total only fifty-eight words—and then the conflict begins.

As you read the following example, look at the expert playwright at work: Exposition is deft, subtle, and quick; basic drives of the characters are immediately shown; the protagonist's goal is clear; the conflict is instantly joined. Those who claim to dislike plot will be hard-pressed to find fault with this structure, yet the technique here is found in many plays.

HERB: Sorry to keep you waiting, Jack. How are you?

(*They shake hands warmly.*)

JACK: I'm fine, Herb.
HERB: Good trip?
JACK: Great.
HERB: I'm damned excited about producing this play of yours.

(*He picks up a manuscript and waves it.*)

The playwright has elected to divide the exposition about the inciting incident into two parts. This is the first mention of one portion of the inciting incident: Jack and Herb have come to an agreement about Herb producing Jack's play. The second portion will be clarified in a few moments.

Note that exposition is brief, subtle, and well crafted to move the action forward while informing the audience of that agreement. Foreshadowing is not a major factor, but "this play of yours" does indicate the object of coming conflict.

Note the importance of visual stage action that neatly replaces several speeches. First, the warm handshake shows the characters' relationship. Second, Herb gestures with the manuscript to reinforce "this play of yours."

The dialogue continues:

JACK: Good.
HERB: Did you order coffee? The girl can get you coffee.
JACK: No, thanks. I just finished breakfast.
HERB: (*Snaps on the intercom on his desk.*) Dorothy?
DOROTHY: (*Her voice is heard.*) Yes, Mr. Miller?

HERB: Any calls?
DOROTHY: No, Mr. Miller.
HERB: I don't want to be disturbed.
DOROTHY: Yes, Mr. Miller.

These brief speeches establish Herb's authority and show the audience that the action takes place in his office. (We might observe that "the *girl* can get you coffee," perhaps not objectionable in 1967 when this play premiered, would offend some audience members today.)

The playwright now shifts to action. In the sequence below, Anderson finishes exposition about the inciting incident (the reference to the agent saying Jack intends what he says in the script), starts the point of attack, establishes the protagonist's goal, and shows the play's conflict. The playwright is shifting from Part One to Part Two.

HERB: (*Sits at the desk.*) Now, Jack . . . I've been talking to that agent of yours, and he says you mean it when you say in your script here . . . (*He reads.*) "Patrick, age forty-three, enters from the bathroom naked."
JACK: Well, sure. It's in the script.
HERB: I know. But I thought maybe it was there just to give an indication for the actor or director.
JACK: No. I mean it.
HERB: Well, Jack . . . I mean, hell! You've written a lot of plays. You know we can't do that.
JACK: Why not?
HERB: We'd be put in jail. You'd offend people.
JACK: Why should people be offended by a naked man?
HERB: Oh, come on . . .
JACK: Damn it, Herb, it's about time our theatre grew up. . . . We've got to let some air in here someplace. . . . It's not as though I were trying to do something sexy. Far from it. . . . Look, when Ibsen put a real-life scene on the stage in 1889, the audience recognized their own lives and stood up and cheered.
HERB: Well, if you put a naked man onstage, they're gonna stand up and go home.

In the next eleven lines Jack says he wants "the audience to get that shock of recognition," as if they're seeing their own lives. The wife is talking to the husband, who is in the bathroom. The husband enters, wet, toothbrush in hand, naked, and says, "Honey, you know I can't hear you when the water's running."

Herb continues to argue and Jack says, "Okay, I'll release you from your contract." That starts the point of attack. Conflicts are joined, the protagonist's goal and the major dramatic question are implied, and the play's action is under way.

Anderson crafts his play to start with action quickly, with action following a brief fourteen-line introductory passage. The playwright hooks the audience immediately with a crisp opening that uses the standard model smoothly and seamlessly.

PART TWO: MIDDLE—
THE PLAY'S STRUGGLES AND ACTION

> *A play is a piece of literature about a section of life written in such a way that it will go over the footlights, in such a way that what it has to say it can say in the theatre. That is the sole test. If it can do this it is a play, good or bad. It is a play insofar as the idea, the content, of it is expressed in theatre terms—the space relationships, the oral values, the personal medium of the actors, and so on—as distinguished from the terms of literature.*
>
> —Stark Young

The middle is the longest and most important part of the play. It begins with the point of attack that starts the conflict, shows the protagonist's goal, contains complications and reversals, and continually builds tensions with forward movement until the height of the tension, or the climax. Part Two is called "rising action," a good description of the desired effect.

Point of Attack

Imagine that a large boulder drops into a calm pond, changing the equilibrium and making a series of active waves that in turn create more waves. That boulder is like a play's point of attack, destroying the existing balance and causing actions that continue throughout the rest of the play.

Importance of the point of attack. Arguably the single most important aspect of plot because it begins the play's action, stimulates the protagonist to drive for a goal, and introduces the play's major dramatic question (MDQ), the point of attack shifts the play from neutral to forward gear. All preceding material is simply introduction and preparation. The point of attack begins Part Two of the play, the struggle and rising action.

For example, in *Hamlet* the point of attack is the Ghost's demand for revenge, which forces Hamlet to take a series of actions that change the balance in the play. The point of attack in *Macbeth* is Macbeth's response to the witches, in the third scene of the first act, who predict he will be king. In *Shock of Recognition* the point of attack is the producer's objection to staging the play with the naked man the playwright wrote. In all cases, the rest of the play consists of struggling to restore balance, and the play ends when that goal is achieved.

How long is the point of attack? Think of sustaining the point of attack so it has adequate intensity to change the course of the play, influence the characters, and communicate to the audience. As a general rule the point of attack may last one or several pages; a single speech is not sufficient.

How do I decide where to place the point of attack? A relatively early point of attack makes your play's beginning more interesting and compelling. "Relatively early" cannot be defined precisely, but a delayed point of attack means the introduction will be filled with exposition, foreshadowing, general mood setting, and the like, which seldom are compelling. The early point of attack in plays as diverse as *Hamlet, Macbeth, Fool for Love, Menagerie,* and *Godot* makes them intensely dramatic plays, in contrast with the delayed point of attack in Euripides' *Medea,* which makes introductory materials extremely long and less interesting for modern audiences.

Early point of attack begins the action quickly. Note how the early point of attack in *The Shock of Recognition* makes the play's action begin crisply and effectively, pulling audience attention into the conflict. Imagine, in contrast, the dull beginning that would have resulted if the playwright had delayed the point of attack by inserting various materials such as exposition, mood-setting, and the like. Anderson could have started his play with telephone conversations between the producer and the playwright's agent ("What do you mean, the playwright wants the play produced exactly as he wrote it?"), dialogue between the producer and his secretary ("Listen, when Jack gets here, I've got to argue with him, so don't let anyone interrupt us," to which she might respond with comments about the binding nature of the producer-playwright contract and the amount of money already invested for the production), and so forth. Those would have substantially delayed the point of attack, weakening the play.

Can my play have more than one point of attack? No. The point of attack begins the action and is the play's first complication.

What characters must be present at the point of attack? The point of attack starts the protagonist into action, striving for his or her goal, which means that character necessarily will be present.

The Protagonist's Goal

In the uneasy balance before the point of attack, the protagonist is static, with no reason to take action. The point of attack gives the protagonist a goal, which provides the action of the rest of the play. For example, the Ghost demands revenge at the point of attack in *Hamlet*. Hamlet, the protagonist, then has a goal: He must first find if the Ghost's story is true, then avenge his father's death. The rest of the play is based on Hamlet's actions to achieve his goal. In *Shock of Recognition* the protagonist's goal is clear: "I want my play performed as I wrote it."

Major Dramatic Question (MDQ)

Elements of plot combine to create the play's action and content. A play's MDQ is a central force that unifies all action and refers to the basic reason you write the play. The MDQ of *A Streetcar Named Desire*, for example, can be simply stated: Can Blanche find the safe haven she must have, at whatever cost to others, if she is to survive? All parts of the play—plot, characterization, meaning—are related to that one issue. The play's action shows Blanche continually working to achieve her goal, in the process endangering her sister's marriage.

Most often implied, not directly stated, the MDQ is posed at the point of attack and directly relates to the protagonist's goal and the play's action and intellectual content. The MDQ is answered at the climax, ending the action. For *Streetcar*, the answer is no.

Blanche is an intruder whose self-interests will damage the Stanley-Stella marriage, and she cannot find the protection she so desperately needs.

The inciting incident, point of attack, and protagonist's goal are linked to the MDQ. *Romeo and Juliet* shows the interrelationship of these aspects of a play. The inciting incident, before the play begins, involves the bitter feud between the Capulets and the Montagues. The point of attack occurs when Romeo Montague and Juliet Capulet fall in love. The protagonist's goal—Romeo wants to marry Juliet—is to find love and happiness through marriage. Obstacles to that goal are vividly clear: the deep-seated active hatred between their families. The play's MDQ thus can be stated: Will the powerful love that Romeo and Juliet share be strong enough to overcome their families' deadly animosities? The play's action involves their increasingly desperate attempts to overcome the families' obstacles and complications. The answer to the MDQ—No, love does not conquer all—is clear in the play's climax.

Do I have to know my play's MDQ before I begin to write? Knowing the play's MDQ is a practical approach for writers who work best when they have a complete scenario of the play, giving them a plan so they know precisely where they are going. Others find that too much careful advance analysis can inhibit the creative process or result in a play that is self-consciously direct. Experience will help you decide what system best fits your working process. Whichever approach you use to write, however, a knowledge of your play's MDQ will be important after you've completed the first draft and begin examining your play for revisions.

How do I know if I have a valid MDQ? An effective MDQ combines the present with a drive to a future and links the inciting incident, point of attack, protagonist's goal, obstacles to that goal, and climax. If you find these elements do not have direct causal relationships, you'll want to examine each carefully, looking for possible revisions that will unify your script.

Complications, Discoveries, Reversals, Obstacles

Complications, discoveries, reversals, and obstacles have distinctive qualities, but their similarities are more important than their differences. We discuss them as "complications." They are the spark plugs that drive your play's motor by changing the course of its action and provoking the characters to respond and change. We noted earlier that the point of attack is the play's first complication, starting the series of dramatic events.

Complications create your play's dramatic tensions by preventing the protagonist from achieving his or her goal. Without them, the protagonist would achieve the goal quickly, easily, and—unfortunately for the play—without conflict and therefore without dramatic values. For example, consider a love story without complications: John wants Sally; she says yes; both sets of parents agree; they marry and live happily ever after. End of play. Bland, isn't it? We see only one aspect of the characters because they face no challenges and have no obstacles to overcome; we know little about their love's nature or size because it is not tested; we discover nothing about the writer's personal attitude about love because no thought is developed; and the plot cannot be sustained because nothing happens.

Instead of that tepid and instantly forgettable love story, think of those you've seen or read such as *Romeo and Juliet*, *Camelot*, *Love Story*, *When Harry Met Sally*, and *Pretty Woman*. Whatever your favorite love story, chances are it attracts you because of the characters' responses to obstacles and complications that impede their love. Those reactions show the depth of their feeling.

"But," "Whoops!" and "Uh-oh." One way to understand the complication is to think of its effects and how it interrupts, cancels, or changes the characters' plans. We can use lighthearted words to show the complication at work. For example, you may find that creating complications is easier if you use the word *whoops!*, as in the example below:

> John talks Sally into eloping, when—*whoops!*—her mother catches them as they're at the door. What will they do next?

Or you may prefer to think of a complication as a *but* factor:

> John wants Sally and they begin plans to marry, *but* her father says no. That changes the course of the action. Now what will John do?

Alternatively, perhaps it will help if you think of a complication as an *uh-oh* event:

> John and Sally are at their wedding rehearsal when—*uh-oh!*—a woman enters, claiming to be John's wife. Now what? How do the characters react to this problem?

Note that complications force the characters to react, making them show other aspects of their characters and becoming more dimensional.

Typical complications affect the protagonist more than other characters. Such complications fall into categories such as:

- Obstacles posed by antagonists who oppose the protagonist
- The protagonist's personal qualities such as shyness, fear, uncertainty, alcoholism, and so forth
- Discoveries about self, others, or significant events such as murder, treachery, and the like
- Supernatural or psychic forces influencing the protagonist's physical or spiritual well-being
- Misunderstandings
- Mistaken identities
- Physical hurdles or barriers that the protagonist must overcome

These complications are new problems the protagonist must attempt to solve to achieve his or her goal.

How many complications must my play have? Your play has at least one complication—the point of attack—or else there'd be no action. A one-act play or short monodrama necessarily has fewer complications than a full-length, and it is difficult to imagine a successful three-act play without a number of major complications per act. There is no minimum or maximum number of complications for a play, but we can suggest that to ensure your play has action you might want to work on the premise that you'll have at least one major complication every five to ten minutes of playing time. Complications can occur almost every minute, illustrated by movies like *Raiders of the Lost Ark*, plays like *Noises Off*, and musicals like *A Funny Thing Happened on the Way to the Forum*.

Entrances Begin Complications

A major character's entrance is a stimulus to the others on stage. An entrance starts a complication that creates a new direction in the play's action. It follows that entrances should have sufficient strength to cause new relationships.

Directors urge playwrights to remember the craft of "building entrances." Playwrights use foreshadowing to prepare the entrance—onstage characters speak anxiously about their concern when the character will arrive—then give the entering person dynamic, elongated action that directly affects the others.

Awareness of stage technique makes you write entrance lines that are long and strong enough to bring the character from the door into the room. A short word or two not only fails to sustain the action but also leaves the character standing helplessly at the entrance, forcing the director to move him or her into the room without motivation.

You've seen effective entrances in musical comedies such as *Hello, Dolly!* and *Mame*, when all characters focus on the sweeping entrance of the star, who often comes down a long staircase while singing and dancing. That same technique is applicable, although used more subtly, in dramas.

For example, note the power of Estelle's entrance in Jean-Paul Sartre's *No Exit* (translated by Stuart Gilbert), a drama about three people who recently died and now are encountering hell. Garcin and Inez are onstage. Sartre constructs Estelle's entrance with tensions between Garcin and Inez, references to suffering and fear, a question ("What's going to happen?"), suspense ("I'm waiting"), pauses, and silences. Estelle enters in the silence.

INEZ: (*Fixing her eyes on him.*) Your mouth!

GARCIN: (*As if wakening from a dream.*) I beg your pardon.

INEZ: Can't you keep your mouth still? You keep twisting it about all the time. It's grotesque.

GARCIN: So sorry. I wasn't aware of it.

INEZ: That's just what I reproach you with. (*GARCIN's mouth twitches.*) There you are! You talk about politeness, and you don't even try to control your face. Remember you're not alone; you've no right to inflict the sight of your fear on me.

GARCIN: (*Getting up and going toward her.*) How about you? Aren't you afraid?

INEZ: What would be the use? There was some point in being afraid *before*; while one still had hope.

GARCIN: (*In a low voice.*) There's no more hope—but it's still "before." We haven't yet begun to suffer.

INEZ: That's so. (*A short silence.*) Well? What's going to happen?

GARCIN: I don't know. I'm waiting.

> (*Silence again.* GARCIN *sits down and* INEZ *resumes her pacing up and down the room.* GARCIN's *mouth twitches; after a glance at* INEZ *he buries his face in his hands. Enter* ESTELLE *with the* VALET. ESTELLE *looks at* GARCIN, *whose face is still hidden by his hands.*)

ESTELLE: (*To* GARCIN.) No! Don't look up! I know what you're hiding with your hands. I know you've no face left. (GARCIN *removes his hands*.) What! (*A short pause. Then, in a tone of surprise.*) But I don't know you.

GARCIN: I'm not the torturer, madam.

ESTELLE: I never thought you were. I—I thought someone was trying to play a rather nasty trick on me. (*To the* VALET.) Is anyone else coming?

VALET: No, madam. No one else is coming.

ESTELLE: Oh! Then we're to stay by ourselves, the three of us, this gentleman, this lady, and myself. (*She starts laughing.*)

GARCIN: (*Angrily.*) There's nothing to laugh about.

ESTELLE: (*Still laughing.*) It's those sofas. They're so hideous. And just look how they've been arranged. It makes me think of New Year's Day—when I used to visit that boring old aunt of mine, Aunt Mary. Her house is full of horrors like that.... I suppose each of us has a sofa of his own. Is that one mine? (*To the* VALET.) But you can't expect me to sit on that one. It would be too horrible for words. I'm in pale blue and it's vivid green.

Note the playwright's skill in giving Estelle a dynamic entrance. She's first horrified to think she knows the man; she has reason to believe he has no face. Then she laughs and talks about sofas, showing a concern about colors that is incongruous in the situation.

Effective Entrances Are Sustained

The entrance continues as Sartre establishes basic parameters of the characters and forthcoming relationships. Inez wants to dominate, Garcin wants to believe he is an intellectual but retreats from confrontations, and Estelle coquettishly focuses on the male, wanting him to serve as a flattering mirror.

Note that an entrance means more than the moment the character enters. The arrival of a new person begins a different series of reactions, which continue for a substantial length of time. Playwrights speak of this as sustaining the effect by making entrances several pages long.

Exits Create Complications

Exits, like entrances, change the dynamics of the situation and characters. An exit usually ends one complication and begins another. Like entrances, exits need to be sustained so they will have sufficient strength, involving both the exiting character and those remaining on stage.

Playwrights with a lively sense of theatre know there is a stage technique for exits, which means giving the exiting character enough lines to move physically from, say, the center of the room to the door. To help the character get to the door, the motivation to exit is begun some speeches earlier. After the character's exit, the playwright then shows the new relationships between those remaining.

For example, note the well-crafted exit of Jim, the Gentleman Caller, in the latter part of *The Glass Menagerie*. Onstage are Jim O'Connor, Amanda Wingfield, and her daughter, Laura; offstage in a nearby room is Amanda's son, Tom. Amanda, the play's protagonist, desperately wants to find someone who will take care of Laura. At Amanda's urging, Tom brought Jim home as a potential suitor for Laura. They've had dinner and Jim and Laura talked. Now hoping a romance is developing between Laura and Jim, she has just gaily said she'll leave the two young folks alone.

JIM: Oh, don't go, Mrs. Wingfield. The fact of the matter is that I've got to be going.

AMANDA: Going, now? You're joking! Why, it's only the shank of the evening, Mr. O'Connor!

JIM: Well, you know how it is.

AMANDA: You mean you're a young workingman and have to keep workingman's hours. We'll let you off early tonight. But only on the condition that next time you stay later. What's the best night for you? Isn't Saturday night the best night for you workingmen?

JIM: I have a couple of time clocks to punch, Mrs. Wingfield. One at morning, another one at night!

AMANDA: My, but you *are* ambitious! You work at night, too?

JIM: No, ma'am, not work but—Betty! (*He crosses deliberately to pick up his hat. The band at the Paradise Dance Hall goes into a tender waltz.*)

AMANDA: Betty? Betty? Who's—Betty!

[Earlier we mentioned that a complication may be an "uh-oh!" factor. Here's an illustration.]

(*There is an ominous cracking sound in the sky.*)

JIM: Oh, just a girl. The girl I go steady with! (*He smiles charmingly. The sky falls.*)

(LEGEND: "THE SKY FALLS.")

AMANDA: Ohhhh . . . Is it a serious romance, Mr. O'Connor?

JIM: We're going to be married the second Sunday in June.

AMANDA: Ohhhh—how nice! Tom didn't mention that you were engaged to be married.

JIM: The cat's not out of the bag at the warehouse yet. You know how they are. They call you Romeo and stuff like that. (*He stops at the oval mirror to put on his hat. He carefully shapes the brim and the crown to give a discreetly dashing effect.*) It's been a wonderful evening, Mrs. Wingfield. I guess this is what they mean by Southern hospitality.

AMANDA: It really wasn't anything at all.

JIM: I hope it don't seem like I'm rushing off. But I promised Betty I'd pick her up at the Wabash depot, an' by the time I get my jalopy down her train'll be in. Some women are pretty upset if you keep 'em waiting.

AMANDA: Yes, I know—the tyranny of women! (*She extends her hand.*) Good-bye, Mr. O'Connor. I wish you luck—and happiness—and success! All three of them, and so does Laura!—Don't you, Laura?

LAURA: Yes!

JIM: (*Taking her hand.*) Good-bye, Laura. I'm certainly going to treasure that souvenir. And don't you forget the good advice I gave you. (*Raises his voice to a cheery shout.*) So long, Shakespeare! Thanks again, ladies—Good night! (*He grins and ducks jauntily out.*)

Note the requirements for an effective exit. Several times before his exit Jim shows his motivation ("I've got to be going"), Amanda's character continues the complication that began with Jim's initial entrance ("on the condition that next time you stay later"), Jim's character concludes that complication (he'll marry someone else "the second Sunday in June"), thus answering the question posed in the play ("Will Amanda find a gentleman caller to marry Laura?"). Those goals accomplished, he leaves.

Williams then shows the changes that are necessary following a character's exit:

> (*Still bravely grimacing,* AMANDA *closes the door on the gentleman caller. Then she turns back to the room with a puzzled expression. She and* LAURA *don't dare to face each other.* LAURA *crouches beside the Victrola to wind it.*)

AMANDA: Things have a way of turning out badly. I don't believe that I would play the Victrola. Well, well—well. Our gentleman caller was engaged to be married! Tom!

The removal of one element of the chemistry creates a new situation. Amanda, who was kittenish and gay in front of the prospective suitor, now is dejected and glum. Her deepest hopes have been dashed.

As the above example from *Menagerie* indicates, exits can add complications to your play's plot and motivate changes in characters. To work effectively, exits should be adequately sustained and given appropriate emotional intensity.

Discoveries Instead of Entrances and Exits

Translate "entrances and exits" to "discoveries" to create different forms of complications that create action without characters entering or leaving the room. The discoveries can be internal, like a Hamlet or Macbeth gaining new personal insight, or they may take the form of one character discovering a fact about someone else; in either case they begin a new course of action. Often the discovery takes place during a conflict, as in Edward Albee's *Who's Afraid of Virginia Woolf?* which is constructed of continual new complications through arguments.

Acts End with Suspense

Crafting the ending of each act in a full-length play requires you to think of your objectives. Usually you want to complete one major action to give the act a feeling of completion. You also consider creating a hook, something that will make the audience want to return after intermission. Usually this involves a form of suspense, perhaps beginning an interesting action that is not completed when the act ends.

Oscar Wilde creates suspense by using ongoing action at the end of the first act of his elegant comedy, *The Importance of Being Earnest*. Jack, you'll recall, uses the name Ernest in town and Jack in the country, which intrigues his friend, Algernon, who wants to find out just what Jack-Ernest is doing. Algernon, in turn, has invented an imaginary person called Bunbury whom he uses as an excuse to get out of other obligations. As Act One ends, Jack gives Gwendolen his address. Algernon smiles to himself and writes the address on his shirt cuff. In a moment Gwendolen exits. Algernon laughs.

JACK: What on earth are you so amused at?
ALGERNON: Oh, I'm a little anxious about poor Bunbury, that's all.
JACK: If you don't take care, your friend Bunbury will get you into a serious scrape some day.
ALGERNON: I love scrapes. They are the only things that are never serious.
JACK: Oh, that's nonsense, Algy. You never talk anything but nonsense.
ALGERNON: Nobody ever does. (*Jack looks indignantly at him, and leaves the room.* ALGERNON *lights a cigarette, reads his shirt-cuff and smiles.*)
Curtain. End of Act One.

Just what is Algernon planning? What will he do with the address? Why does he smile? Wilde ends Act One by beginning an action that is designed to make the audience want to return for

Act Two to find out how that action will conclude. The audience likely has a good idea what Algernon will do, and they look forward to enjoying the delicious fun with him.

Climax

The climax is the highest point in the dramatic series of events. It shows the outcome of complications, completes the action, and answers the MDQ posed at the point of attack. The protagonist's goal is complete, meeting success or failure, and an equilibrium is restored. Every scene and incident of the play builds to this point. For the audience member, the climax brings a satisfying feeling that all is logically complete. The climax is inherent in the play's beginning; climax and point of attack are like two bookends that are causally related and encompass the play.

The climax in plays such as *Hamlet* and *Macbeth* occurs at the deaths of Hamlet and Macbeth, but playwrights shouldn't conclude that a climax requires death. In *Death of a Salesman*, for example, the climax is not the death of Willy Loman but instead is Willy's discovery that his son Biff loves him. In other plays there may be a wedding or comparable satisfactory outcome to the protagonist's goal.

Climax answers the MDQ. Think of the climax as the answer to the major dramatic question that was asked at the point of attack: "Will Hamlet avenge his father's death?" "What will be the result of Macbeth's quest for power?" "Will Amanda find a way to protect Laura's uncertain future?"

Should I know my play's climax before I begin writing? Some playwrights say they write better when they don't know where the play will go. These writers start at the beginning without a plan and write through the play, finding the climax when they get there. On the other hand, many playwrights believe they cannot write until they know the climax and they won't begin writing the play until they know its destination. Control of the climax—some complete it before beginning other scenes—allows them to construct their plays backward from that point, making certain that all action leads to the climax. Arthur Miller, for example, started *Death of a Salesman* with only one firm idea: Loman was to destroy himself, motivated by his memories. All the rest of the play, Miller says, was determined by that climax. Of the two techniques, the latter's logical efficiency is more appealing and therefore has practical values for beginning playwrights.

PART THREE: ENDING—A SENSE OF FINALITY

You cannot say . . . that such and such is not a play because it violates the unities or is in one long act or has a speech of ten pages' length. But you can say, for example, that when a dramatist—as I remember to have seen once in a manuscript . . . writes that the heroine turns and walks out the door at the back of the room and as she reaches it smiles a radiant, happy smile, he may be writing fiction but is not writing in theatre terms, since the audience could not see at all the smile, which therefore as theatre it does not exist.

—Stark Young

Your play ends with the event that concludes the action; the conflict is resolved; the story does not require any further action or explanation. Your goal in Part Three is to complete the play so it ends rather than stops—and, further, so it ends *once*, without false endings. Part Three is falling action or resolution, containing the denouement and catharsis, and restoring the play to an equilibrium.

Deus ex Machina

Deus ex machina is not properly a part of plot—some would say it is not part of a proper plot—but we discuss it here to help you avoid its dangers. Literally "god from the machine," the term refers to a device found in the climax of some Greek tragedies when a cranelike machine lowered a god down to the stage. Unable to resolve the plot, the playwright brings on a god to solve problems.

To modern tastes that device sounds impossibly quaint and old-fashioned. Nonetheless, the artifice continues today. For example, those who remember the Perry Mason television program aren't likely to forget each show's *deus ex machina* device: In the last minutes of the show, just when Mason's client appeared most guilty, a stranger in the courtroom would stand and confess to the crime. Most often such lack of motivation is comic.

In modern plays *deus ex machina* refers to any character or action artificially imposed into the play to bring it to a conclusion. It is a mark of poor writing. Avoid the device by maintaining strict quality control over causal relationships, plot construction, and character motivations.

Denouement

The denouement is the final knitting together of loose ends. If you write a climax that completes the major questions, the denouement can be quite short. For example, there are only nine speeches in the denouement of *Hamlet*. It reestablishes order and balance to the universe of the play.

Denouement in modern theatre tends to be brief, avoiding any appearance of knitting together the loose ends. Many of today's playwrights write analogies or implications, challenging the audience to consider possible solutions to the dilemmas the play presents. This technique is perhaps best represented by the final lines and stage direction that end Samuel Beckett's *Waiting for Godot*:

ESTRAGON: Well, shall we go?
VLADIMIR: Yes, let's go.

They do not move.

Curtain. End of play.

Catharsis

Catharsis is not well understood and is often subject to some mild controversy in theatre circles. The concept begins with Aristotle's *Poetics* in which he says that a play should allay the emotions it arouses. Some modern playwrights find the idea troublesome. One wonders if the Greek concept of catharsis—often called ending a play with a purging of the audience's emotions—can be understood fully in today's theatre. We can appreciate the term in a distant intellectual way, but can we relate to it emotionally? Have modern audiences experienced so many dramatic stories (plays, movies, television shows) that we are more "story sophisticated" than the Greeks? If so, our emotive connections to theatre may be less than the Greek audience's response, exemplified when "strong men fainted and women miscarried" at one particularly dramatic moment. Are today's audiences capable of such response? The

Greeks apparently needed a catharsis so they would not take home with them the anguish they felt at the drama. Do we? It is an interesting argument, one you may wish to examine as part of your development as a playwright.

Catharsis may be better understood as the conclusion of the emotional aspects of the action and characters. Viewed this way it is more an aspect of the playwright's craft and less dependent on audience response. If you write a conclusion that finishes the movement and evolution of the characters, you'll also satisfy audience needs.

The O. Henry Ending

The short story writer O. Henry (pen name of William Sydney Porter) was best known for sentimental stories with surprise twist endings, exemplified by "The Gift of the Magi," which deals with a poverty-stricken couple, each determined to buy the other a Christmas present. They have no money, only the husband's gold watch and the wife's luxuriously long hair. It ends with a typical surprise: The husband sells his watch to buy her a set of combs for her beautiful hair; she sells her hair to buy him a watch fob.

The best advice to a playwright planning a twist ending is simple: Don't. The device is O. Henry's trademark, and imitations lack his individualistic style. If the trick succeeds at all, it works only with quite short pieces. Finally, such gimmick endings are implausible and play a trick on the audience, which won't appreciate being the butt of the writer's joke. Avoid O. Henry endings if you want your plays to be produced.

Playwright's Curtain Speech

Some playwrights believe they must write a final speech that sums up the play's meaning. Avoid the temptation. (Or write it if you must, but throw it away afterward.) Instead, make certain that the play's action expresses its meaning. If it does, no curtain speech is necessary; if it doesn't, no curtain speech will correct the problem.

EXERCISES USING OTHER PLAYS

1. Teaching others about plot can enhance your own understanding and comprehension. Ask a friend or relative to be your

student. First, assign him or her to read a play in which plot elements are clear. Then go through the play identifying and explaining the following terms:

Plot
Present tense versus past tense; sense of future
Inciting incident
Exposition
Foreshadowing
Setting a mood
Sense of equilibrium
Point of attack
Protagonist's goal
Protagonist's plan
Major dramatic question
Complications
Climax
Deus ex machina
Denouement
Catharsis
Playwright's curtain speech

2. Work with a fellow playwright to define the above terms and find them in a play such as *Hamlet, Macbeth,* or any other of your choosing.

EXERCISES FOR THE PLAY YOU ARE WRITING

Answers to these exercises should be entered in your writer's journal.

1. Describe the inciting incident that sparks your play. When did it happen? How will that incident influence the protagonist? Who was involved in the inciting incident?
2. How will the protagonist discover the importance of the inciting incident? What is his or her response?
3. Decide to use foreshadowing in your play's beginning. Write several instances of foreshadowing.
4. Write a brief narrative that describes the exposition the audience must know. Decide the barest essentials you'll use in

the play's beginning. Plan when you'll use the rest of the exposition later in the play.

5. Outline your play's point of attack. How does it link with the inciting incident? What characters are present? Identify the cause of the point of attack (that is, protagonist discovers significant information, major demands are placed on the protagonist, and so forth). Write as much of the point of attack as you can, using dialogue and action.

6. Describe the protagonist's goal. What motivates him or her to achieve that goal? What is the protagonist's emotional involvement in the goal? What is the character's plan?

7. What stops the protagonist from achieving the goal? Who opposes him or her? Why? List a number of complications and obstacles. What are the protagonist's emotional reactions to each obstacle?

8. Put the obstacles in the order they'll occur during the play.

9. Describe the climax of the play you are going to write. Does the protagonist get his or her goal? Does the play end "upbeat" or "down"? Be detailed.

10. Show the interrelationship of your play's inciting incident, point of attack, protagonist's goal, major dramatic question, and climax. You may wish to create a diagram to show how these fit together.

A good story is obviously a difficult thing to invent, but its difficulty is a poor reason for despising it. It should have coherence and sufficient probability for the needs of the theme; it should be of a nature to display the development of character . . . and it should have completeness, so that when it is finally unfolded no more questions can be asked about the persons who take part in it. It should have like Aristotle's tragedy a beginning, a middle, and an end.
—W. Somerset Maugham

7

Constructing Dialogue: Action Through Words

The ear is an essential quality of the dialogue-writer, the ear that can catch and reproduce the tone of characters' speech.... Really good dialogue is not what it would be in life; it can only seem to sound as if it were. No stage bore can be boring the way a real life bore is. He would bore the audience, too.

JOHN VAN DRUTEN

Your characters talk.

Is dialogue nothing more than people talking? Hardly.

George Bernard Shaw, with characteristic trenchant wit (and equally characteristic lack of modesty), points out that if his plays are "merely talk" then Beethoven's symphonies are "merely music." Shaw accurately indicates the complex qualities of dialogue. Being a playwright requires mastering the art of writing dialogue, which is much more than people talking. Directors notice your play's dialogue first, before plot and characters become visible, and you want to earn their favorable attention by constructing dialogue that has the same vitality and animation that you give characters and plot.

When your dialogue succeeds, the result is exciting. Hearing your dialogue on stage, delivered by talented actors and communicating effectively to an audience, is a thrilling reward that essayists, poets, and novelists can never experience.

WHAT IS DIALOGUE?

A preliminary definition helps us start this chapter's exploration of the many dimensions of dialogue: *Through speeches and silences, what is spoken and deliberately unspoken, dialogue is the action that characters do, expressing conflict of people working at cross-purposes.* For example, both verbal and physical action are present in the famous "nose" scene in the first act of Edmond Rostand's *Cyrano de Bergerac.* Cyrano eloquently mocks Valvert's lack of imagination in saying "Your nose is rather large," then duels with him while simultaneously composing a ballade—"Then, as I end the refrain, thrust home!"

Expect some mild confusion about terms referring to characters' speeches. Theatre workers often use "dialogue," "speech," and "lines" synonymously, although the first word refers to the playwright's written script and the latter two are actors' terms. Some directors and playwrights also think of dialogue as "diction," a term that reflects the Aristotelian division of drama into six elements (that is, plot, character, thought, diction, music, and spectacle). Although theatrical dialogue means "dramatic exchanges expressing conflict between two or more characters," common theatre practice also applies the word to monologues, soliloquies, and speeches in one-person monodramas.

THEATRICAL DIALOGUE DIFFERS FROM OTHER FORMS OF WRITING

Stageworthy dialogue is similar to, yet different from, speeches or dialogue in novels. As a writer you necessarily respect language and fundamental principles of good writing, such as concern for emphasis through sentence structure, use of active instead of passive voice, and appropriate word choice. As a playwright, however, you freely break writing rules to achieve theatrical effect. We can envy Lewis Carroll's egg's arrogant freedom to make words his slave—" 'When *I* use a word,' Humpty Dumpty said in a rather scornful tone, 'it means just what I choose it to mean, neither more nor less' "—but when *we* use a word it means what the audience thinks it means, and we'd better be certain we're communicating accurately.

Most of us have three vocabularies: the spoken (the smallest vocabulary), the heard (second largest), and the read (largest). Theatrical dialogue typically uses the first two vocabularies; formal or literary writing, in contrast, involves the third. Some playwrights, perhaps interested in proving their literacy, depend heavily on the third vocabulary, and their plays contain dialogue that is stiff, stilted, distant from humanity, or even full of quotations from poems or essays. Expect directors to reject such plays.

Theatrical Dialogue Versus Life's Conversations

Theatrical dialogue differs radically from life's "conversations," "discussions," "chats," or comparable words that suggest idle, emotionless, rambling, disorganized, ordinary talk. Those qualities do not make effective dialogue for the stage. Thinking that your characters converse or talk is a red danger flag indicating you're missing the essentials of dramatic writing, which is carefully selected, individualized, condensed, shaped, and organized for characters and plot. Although you seek to evoke the flavor of the way people talk in real life so your characters will appear real, you never replicate real-life chats and instead construct their dialogue to achieve dramatic tensions and conflicts.

Theatrical Dialogue Versus Writing for Novels

Theatrical dialogue differs from dialogue found in many novels. From your reading you know that some novelists write long, rambling speeches or lengthy descriptions as if the other players in the story somehow temporarily disappeared from the scene; novelists may use inverted or convoluted sentences on the premise that the reader has the option of rereading the passage to find its sense; and novelists can write words, figures of speech, or literary allusions that require the reader to consult a dictionary or a literary concordance.

Such writing techniques, perhaps acceptable in novels, are ineffective in the theatre. Ernest Hemingway said that the novelist is engaged in a perpetual battle to craft the perfect sentence; the playwright, in contrast, is less concerned with individual written sentences and more interested in oral communication of the entire story. You're like a storyteller crafting suspense and illuminating mysteries to a group sitting around the campfire, and every aspect of your story must be clear and interesting to everyone, aimed at neither the elite nor the unsophisticated.

Theatrical Dialogue Versus Literary Writing

"Dialogue in this play sounds like literary writing," a producer or director may say about a play. It is no compliment. Often the comment explains why a play is rejected.

Theatrical dialogue is an artistic reproduction of the way particular characters speak, designed for actors to speak and aimed at the audience's ear, in contrast to literary writing which is more formal, written for an individual reader's eye. When appropriate to the character and situation, theatrical dialogue uses incomplete sentences, incorrect grammar, informal style, slang, and profanity. As a playwright your first priority is dramatic characterization and action—your dialogue shows characters in action, the opposite of a literary essayist dispassionately commenting on life.

Theatrical Dialogue Versus Screen Writing

Screenwriters and playwrights share common bonds. Both are storytellers who depend on conflict for dramatic impact, seek to give artistic representations of life, use similar plot and characterization techniques, and write within the same mandate to "show, not tell." They differ in the amount they use dialogue and visual images. Screen writing, whether for television or movies, depends on visual images more than dialogue; the playwright, in contrast, depends on dialogue more than visual communications.

Theatrical Dialogue Versus Speech Writing

Stageworthy dialogue is like speech in that both are forms of oral communication that is directed at the auditor's ear, but it differs from speech in a number of significant aspects. Speech often is oratorical and follows rhetorical rules, which makes it similar to literary writing, and it usually informs or exhorts listeners to take action. Theatrical dialogue, in contrast, is an exchange of sharply contrasting views between more than one person, and there is no explicit call for action.

Debate, an organized form of speech, presents ideas in a logical point-counterpoint system, a coolly analytical attitude ill-suited to dramatic writing, which is full of fiery statements by opinionated individualists who won't let an opponent develop a counterargument. As a playwright, think of yourself as one who shows humans in action, not as a politician or member of the clergy who makes speeches about issues.

THE PLAYWRIGHT'S GOALS

Effective dialogue must serve many masters. You seek to create dialogue that expresses the play's action and conflict, brings the characters into sharp focus, informs the audience of situation and focuses its imagination to the play's theme, communicates the play's tone, and contributes to the play's aesthetic appeal.

Tensions and Actions

Effective dialogue is full of tension, like spiritual and psychological rubber bands stretching to a snapping point, showing conflict and people working at cross-purposes, characters' emotional involvement in issues highly important to them, and vital disagreements. Edward Albee's *Who's Afraid of Virginia Woolf?* illustrates dialogue's tensions and actions. At one point Martha goads George into attacking her, and they wrestle to the floor while Honey shouts "Violence! Violence!" Nick pulls George off. George regains his composure and says, "We've played Humiliate the Host," and then asks what other games they can play: "How about . . . how about . . . Hump the Hostess? HUNH?? How about that? How about Hump the Hostess? *(To Nick.)* You wanna play that one? You wanna play Hump the Hostess? HUNH? HUNH?" Seeing George's desperation, Martha says scornfully, "Portrait of a man drowning."

Dialogue Is Action

Active and vital dialogue thrusts your play forward as much as active and vital character and plot give the play forward momentum; passive or inactive dialogue slows the play's pace no less than passive or inactive character and plot. Harold Pinter's *The Dumbwaiter* deals with two professional killers arguing over apparently inconsequential matters because they are increasingly nervous as they wait for their victim to enter. They become involved in a power struggle. Ben tells Gus to light the kettle to make tea. Gus says no one can light a kettle; Ben must mean light the gas. BEN *(powerfully):* "If I say go and light the kettle, I mean go and light the kettle." GUS: "How can you light a kettle?" BEN: "It's a figure of speech! Light the kettle! It's a figure of speech!" GUS: "I've never heard it." BEN: "Who's the senior partner here, me or you?" GUS: "You." BEN: *(vehemently):* "Nobody says light the gas!

What does the gas light?" GUS: "What does the gas—?" BEN: *(grabbing him with two hands by the throat, at arm's length)*: "THE KETTLE, YOU FOOL!"

Dialogue Makes Emotional Appeal

Dialogue conveys characters' emotions and awakens comparable feelings in the audience. "Pray you, undo this button," Lear says in the heartwrenching conclusion of *King Lear*. At the end of Tennessee Williams's *A Streetcar Named Desire* a doctor leads Blanche from the home of Stanley and Stella; Blanche has one of theatre's most poignant speeches that sums up her character: "Whoever you are—I have always depended on the kindness of strangers." Act One of Beth Henley's *The Wake of Jamey Foster* ends with Marshael Foster, the new widow, in despair: "I don't know how I'm gonna get through this night. I can't imagine ever seeing the morning."

Dialogue Expresses Playwright's Credo

Dialogue can express the personal beliefs that led you to write your play. In Arthur Miller's *Death of a Salesman*, Biff sums up his father: "He had the wrong dreams. All, all, wrong. The man didn't know who he was." William Saroyan's *My Heart's in the Highlands* shows people attempting to cope with poverty, old age, and a world at war, concluding with Johnny's speech: "I'm not mentioning any names, Pa, but something's wrong somewhere."

Dialogue Implies Theme

Although you do not want to express your play's theme explicitly—a direct statement violates theatre's "show, don't tell" prime directive—you can imply it with subtle dialogue. *Hamlet* contains the well-known statement that describes the play's focus: "Something is rotten in the state of Denmark," followed by a less known but more significant line: "But Heaven will set it right." Rebecca in Thornton Wilder's *Our Town* shows the play's concern with universal truths when she says Jane Crofut received a letter addressed to her: "Jane Crofut; The Crofut Farm; Grover's Corners; Sutton County; New Hampshire; United States of America." Asked what's unusual about that, she adds that the envelope's address also included: "Continent of North America; the Earth; the Solar System; the Universe; the Mind of God."

Dialogue Shows the Play's Tone

Joe in William Saroyan's *The Time of Your Life* expresses the play's warmth when he talks about the marriage that he almost had and all the imagined kids, adding: "My favorite was the third one." Also in the play is an Arab who sits alone at the bar and from time to time says nothing more than two words that express the bewildering mysteries of human behavior: "No foundation." At a telling moment he expands on his idea by adding six words: "No foundation—all the way down the line." Dialogue in Oscar Wilde's comedy, *The Importance of Being Earnest*, shows the light-spirited tone with serious references to consumption of delicacies (ALGERNON: "Why is it that in a bachelor's establishment the servants invariably drink the champagne? I ask merely for information." LANE: I attribute it to the superior quality of the wine, sir. I have often observed that in married households the champagne is rarely of a first-rate brand") and light snacks (ALGERNON: "Have some bread and butter. The bread and butter is for Gwendolen. Gwendolen is devoted to bread and butter").

Dialogue Stimulates Audience's Imagination

Theatre becomes more effective when it awakens the audience's imagination. In Sam Shepard's *Fool for Love*, for example, the Old Man (visible only to Eddie and the audience but not to others in the play) shows the power of the mind when dealing with love. He tells Eddie to look at a picture on the wall, although no picture is present: "Barbara Mandrell. That's who that is. Barbara Mandrell. You heard a' her?" Eddie says he has. "Well," says the Old Man, "Would you believe me if I told ya' I was married to her?" Eddie says no. "Well, see, now that's the difference right there. That's realism. I am actually married to Barbara Mandrell in my mind. Can you understand that?"

Dialogue Reflects Characters: Characters Create Dialogue

Dialogue and characterization are like love and marriage: Dialogue creates characters, and characters create dialogue. One secret for a successful marriage can be stated simply: Create characters who are compelled to say what you need them to say.

Ineffective dialogue makes characters sound stilted, bland, emotionless, uninterested and uninteresting, or oratorical. Effective theatrical dialogue brings characters to life by giving them tensions, obstacles, unique emotions, vitality, and dedication to achieving their goals. In Eugene O'Neill's *The Hairy Ape* the protagonist is Yank, a fireman on an ocean liner. He discovers that a beautiful female passenger called him an ape who made her sick when she saw him working at the ship's boilers: "Yuh tink I made her sick too, do yuh? Just lookin' at me, huh? Hairy ape, huh? *(In a frenzy of rage.)* I'll fix her! I'll tell her where to git off! She'll git down on her knees and take it back or I'll bust de face offen her!"

Dialogue Shows Characterization

Dialogue shows your characters' individual personalities and powerful needs, relationships, beliefs, thoughts, and emotions. Often a simple speech shows the inner workings of the mind: When Macbeth tells his wife that King Duncan will arrive at their castle this night, she responds, "And when goes hence?" Four words show wheels busily turning in Lady Macbeth's mind, plans and connivances that express her character and imply forthcoming bleak actions. Macbeth later shows that in freely taking others' lives as if they were worthless he has unwittingly made his own as meaningless: "Life's but a walking shadow, a poor player/That struts and frets his hour upon the stage,/And then is heard no more: it is a tale/Told by an idiot, full of sound and fury,/Signifying nothing."

Dialogue Captures and Shows Character's Unique Qualities

Dialogue is like a fingerprint, unique for each character in your play. In this sense you apply what you learn from listening carefully to friends, relatives, and public officials. Each individual's oral style, word choice, and sentence structure makes him or her immediately identifiable. For example, as satirists and comics demonstrate, even casual followers of politics readily recognize the phraseology and style of a Dwight Eisenhower, John F. Kennedy, Lyndon Johnson, Richard Nixon, Ronald Reagan, George Bush, Dan Quayle, Mario Cuomo, and Ross Perot.

Imagine that someone has transcribed an intense argument among your mother, father, and friend or spouse. You receive a typed copy of that scene but minus identifying names. You could identify each speaker by his or her particular emphases, use of words, and sentence structure. Likewise, all of your play's characters, or at least each major character, need individualistic dialogue.

For example, the characters in Beth Henley's *The Wake of Jamey Foster* have individual concerns and personalities expressed through dialogue. Katty speaks primarily about her clothing; Wayne's dialogue shows he focuses on presenting what he believes is an appropriate "image" or correct behavior; Brocker's speeches are earthy; and Pixrose is preoccupied with arson.

Dialogue Makes Characters Easily Recognizable

Directors explaining a negative reaction to a play's dialogue may use the phrase, "The characters all speak with the same tongue." They expect each character to have a unique, personalized tongue. When you succeed in creating speech patterns distinct for each character, someone reading the play can recognize each speaker by dialogue alone. The alternative, never recommended, is for each character to sound alike, usually like the playwright, thereby eliminating individuality.

Think of the highly individualized dialogue of Stanley versus Blanche in Tennessee Williams's *A Streetcar Named Desire*. Each has distinctive rhythms and words. Perhaps more important, each has highly individualized topics—Blanche talks about her appearance and ethereal subjects; Stanley speaks of raw, animalistic self-concerns.

Individuality comes with knowledge of the characters. The better you know the characters, the more you'll achieve the elusive goal of individualistic speech patterns. Contrasts are helpful for many plays: Think of each character as having a widely different background, education, environment, and employment. Helpful, too, is giving each character distinctly different emotional and intellectual qualities, ambitions and dreams, reactions to stimuli, and vocabulary. You'll discover a serendipity factor: As you continually seek to create distinctive dialogue for each character, he or she will take on added dimension, energy, and individuality.

ACQUIRING AN EAR FOR DIALOGUE

Earlier chapters discussed the "writer's eye" for dramatic action and characters. Here we discuss what playwright John Van Druten says is an equally important imaginative tool: your "writer's ear" for dialogue to communicate your vision from the page to the stage through the actors to the audience. Effective dialogue requires the playwright to have a love for words and the way words mix to construct ideas that depict characters. An ear for language hears vitality, rhythm, word choice, speech patterns, images, and brevity. Four basic sources can help you improve your ear for dialogue.

Life

You can train your ear by learning from life, listening carefully to speech patterns of people around you, recognizing unusual qualities, and noting how each individual expresses emotions and thoughts through unique word choice, rhythm, and sentence structure. Because you're most interested in dramatic values, be especially attentive to people in conflict over desires, ideas, and needs. Just as painters fill sketch pads with bits and pieces of anatomy or landscapes that can be used for their paintings, fill your writer's notebook with oral sketches that may later become part of a character in a play.

Actors

A second way to train your ear is to ask actors to read your play while you listen carefully to the dialogue, perhaps closing your eyes to concentrate more fully on the lines. Do they have to pause for breath in the middle of sentences? Try writing simple, declarative sentences. Do they stumble over unfamiliar terms? Consider substituting better known words. Do you hear words blending together because terminal sounds are followed by similar sounds ("seems simple," "cook can," and the like)? See if you can recast the sentence. Does the dialogue sound like ordinary chat? Construct conflict that shows characters working against each other. It's a good idea to experiment with changing lines so you can hear the importance of rhythm, sentence structure, word choice, and images. Actors' comments and suggestions may help you strengthen your dialogue.

Other Playwrights

You can improve your ear for dialogue by studying other playwrights, attending plays in production or rehearsals, and listening to the way the dialogue is constructed. Careful play reading will sharpen your ear and increase your ability to distinguish between effective and ineffective dialogue. Some playwrights believe they learn to improve their writing skills by copying word for word other playwrights' excellent dialogue passages, not to imitate but to discover firsthand how superior dialogue is constructed.

The Character and Your Imagination

Dialogue springs from characters. Playwrights train themselves to "listen" to what each character wants to say and the unique way he or she says it. Your goal is to be sure all characters are vital and alive: When one character is talking, focus your writer's ear on the others and demand they respond. You'll find that dialogue is improved if you create characters who are so different from one another that they necessarily have different speech patterns; alternatively (or simultaneously), force characters to have different ways of expressing themselves so they'll be dramatic opposites.

Avoid Examples of Poor Dialogue

Not all examples of dialogue will help you develop your ear. Avoid inferior dialogue, such as that often found on television's daytime soaps. Your ear is ill-served by their rambling sentences, over-ripe and unmotivated emotions, junk words, halting speeches, repetitions, and dependency on camera tricks or sound effects to add snap and crackle to anemic lines. You don't need such qualities infecting your ear for dialogue.

COMMUNICATING BASIC DETAILS

Plays must be complete and self-contained. You use dialogue and action, not printed programs or the like, to communicate all necessary basic information to the audience. Names, situations, and relationships are the foundation stones for the play's shape and construction; and without knowledge of such fundamental materials the audience may not be drawn into the characters and situations. The larger the number of characters, and the more complex the situation, the greater effort you'll have to make to help the audience know the essential details.

Dialogue Communicates
Facts, Names, and Relationships

The passage below illustrates the playwright's use of dialogue to convey basic information immediately to the audience. Note that in just a few moments the audience knows the characters' names, differences in their attitudes, and certain details about their respective pasts. Strokes of foreshadowing indicate an ominous future. The play begins with these lines:

CLIFF: *(Opening door.)* Ralph? Is that you? Good Lord, what are you doing here this time of . . .

RALPH: *(Entering.)* I'm driving by on my way home, see your lights on, and I say to myself, "Self," I say, "Self, Cliffie-boy is still up. Let's say hey to good old Cliff." So, hey, Cliff.

CLIFF: *(Weakly.)* Hey, Ralph.

RALPH: *(Active, looking around room, busy.)* Ain't seen you, been a while, right? Like maybe, what, six years? Didn't you know they let me out a few weeks ago? I surely thought my old buddy Clifford W. Carpenter would look me up real fast.

CLIFF: Look, it's late and I've got a busy day tomorrow. . . .

RALPH: Hard to find you. Went to your old dump and they told me you'd moved, no forwarding address.

CLIFF: Yeah, well . . . So, how have you been?

RALPH: *(As before.)* Pretty slick, this place. Books, paintings, wall-to-wall carpet, silver in the cabinet. Man, you doin' okay for a guy who six years ago didn't have more'n fifty bucks at one time.

CLIFF: Ralph, you live, what? Twenty, twenty-five miles away?

RALPH: *(A large smile.)* You know where I live, huh?

CLIFF: I mean, what's this about just passing by?

RALPH: *(Waving his hand vaguely.)* Old buddies got to keep in touch. You 'n' me, we gotta catch up. Let's you and me get a drink outta your fancy bar and we'll bullshit about the good old times when we used to go huntin', chasin' girls, and raisin' hell.

CLIFF: *(Hesitantly.)* Ralph . . . Not a drink. Not since they put you in . . .

RALPH: *(Quickly.)* Hey, I'm cool, pal. On the wagon. This here's solid-citizen Ralph Thomas McQuire, no warrants outstanding, all bills paid to society. But you don't have to worry about society asking you to pay up, do you?

CLIFF: *(Looking at watch.)* I'd like to talk but . . .

RALPH: *(He puts his hand in his coat pocket. There is a large bulge.)*
Just a couple minutes, Cliffie-boy.
CLIFF: *(Apprehensively, looking at the bulge.)* Now look, Ralph . . .
RALPH: We'll catch up on things, have one drink for old times. I
thought 'bout you a lot, my old, old friend. I missed you. Six
years, looking at the sun through them damned bars, I missed
you. *(Smiling.)* Yeah, ol' buddy, we're gonna catch up.

The "Rule of Three" Ensures Communication

How can you be confident that the audience knows vital factual
information such as names, relationships, situation, conflicts, and
the like? Professional playwrights emphasize a rule of three, by
which they mean giving the audience important information at
least three times. This rule, more pragmatic than philosophical,
is based on an awareness that the audience may have problems
hearing and comprehending specific details that are mentioned
only once.

Note the application of the rule of three in the above Cliff-Ralph
scene. Facts are repeated: characters' names, the late hour, implications about where Ralph has been, statements regarding six
years (made significant in Ralph's last speech), and suggestions
that Ralph may have a problem with alcohol. Different vocal patterns emphasize the contrast between the two characters.

The rule of three also applies to plot and thought. In the Cliff-
Ralph scene there are repeated units of foreshadowing that indicate a troubled relationship, starting with Ralph entering without
invitation, allusions to Ralph searching for Cliff who seems reluctant to be found, suggestions that Cliff has more money now than
he did six years ago, and especially the repeated "old buddy" lines.

Effective use of the rule of three calls for deft and subtle writing.
You want to hide the technique—dialogue will sound strained if
the audience recognizes the device at work—and characters must
have clear motivation for each repetition. Common sense tells you
not to use names too often because that violates the way people
speak and, further, would quickly become singsong. The theatre
artisan will use indirect restatement more than word-for-word
repetition.

Specifics Communicate
More Thoroughly than Abstracts

Specific references—explicit names, locations, facts—help the audience relate to the character and situation. For example, Jane Martin's monodrama *Twirler* focuses on a young lady's experience as a baton twirler. Martin could have written that the character's mother sent her for baton twirling lessons and let it go at that, but instead she uses concrete, specific references that give the dialogue immediacy and meaning: "Momma hit the daily double on horses named Spin Dry and Silver Revolver, and she said that was a sign so she gave me lessons at the Dainty Deb Dance Studio where the lady, Miss Aurelia, taught some twirling on the side."

Equally, the playwright might have said that the twirler had an accident, but Martin again uses the specific: "Oh, I've flown high and known tragedy both. My daddy says it's put spirit in my soul and steel in my heart. My left hand was crushed in a riding accident by a horse named Big Blood Red, and though I came back to twirl I couldn't do it at the highest level. That was denied me by Big Blood Red who clipped my wings." The specific references themselves convey an elevated feeling like poetry, giving your dialogue (and your character) added sparkle and meaning.

Pronouns Weaken Communication

Just as specific references are valuable because they communicate basic details and a sense of place, pronouns are remarkably anemic in theatrical dialogue because they lack specificity. Although you don't want to fall into the trap of unnecessary repetition, you'll find that repeating the noun is usually more effective: "Big Blood Red" is stronger than "he." Furthermore, antecedents may be lost (the novel's reader can skim backward to find the reference noun, but the listener cannot). Examine your dialogue for references to he, she, they, and it, and substitute proper names or nouns if there's any chance of confusion or if the specific conveys more power.

TECHNIQUES OF WRITING DIALOGUE

I love plays where there is actually style in the language. I like plays that have a sense of language that is exact and exciting, almost pristine in its simplicity. A play's language

should have an inevitable musicality that leads to the play's
emotional and intellectual center.

—Linda Hunt

It's the way the playwright thinks, the imagery, the metaphor,
his or her sense of theatre, that makes me want to do a play.

—Hume Cronyn

Actors such as Linda Hunt, winner of an Academy Award for
The Year of Living Dangerously, and Hume Cronyn, who has appeared in many plays and films, frequently with his wife, Jessica
Tandy, reflect opinions of many other actors: They are attracted
to working in a play on the strength of its language and theatrical
metaphor. Directors, actors, and producers look for plays that are
written for the stage, that is, with theatrical images such as action,
characters in motion, visual qualities, and most especially dialogue that is of and for the theatre.

Ellipsis: The Unfinished Thought

You've seen the ellipsis in formal writing to indicate missing material in a quotation, but in dramatic dialogue the ellipsis indicates
a character's unspoken thoughts or words. (Some playwrights prefer to use dashes instead of dots, as illustrated later in an example
from Shaw's *Candida.*) Perhaps the character is unwilling to face
a blunt truth, or he or she may be hesitant to offend another
character. Sometimes the character may struggle for words. You'd
write such dialogue like this:

BILL: I think I'll . . . Or maybe not.
ANNE: If you don't do what he said as soon as . . . your father said
he'd . . .
BILL: Yes, but . . . No. I won't do it!

Ellipses quickly can become overused—the above example probably has too much cagey nonstatement—but when properly used
the device can show each character's emotional and mental state.

Making Clear the Unfinished Thought

Ellipses or incomplete sentences may confuse actors, making them
search for the missing meaning and perhaps coming to incorrect

conclusions. To ensure clarity, you can indicate the unspoken completion of the sentence. Armed with that knowledge, actors can use vocal techniques to communicate the unspoken to the audience. For example, in *Agnes of God*, John Pielmeier uses the standard series of dots to indicate the ellipses, then adds a parenthetical note to explain to the actor the rest of the sentence (which is not spoken):

DOCTOR: *(Laughing)* You're as crazy as the rest of your family.
MOTHER: I don't know if it's true, I . . . (only think it might be possible).
DOCTOR: How?
MOTHER: I don't . . . (know).
DOCTOR: Do you think a big white dove came flying through her window?
MOTHER: No, I can't believe that.
DOCTOR: That would be a little scary, wouldn't it? Second Coming Stopped by Hysterical Nun.
MOTHER: This is *not* the Second Coming, Doctor Livingstone. Don't misunderstand me.
DOCTOR: But you just said . . . (there isn't any father).

The above example also indicates another device to enliven dialogue: the Doctor's satirical newspaper headline ("Second Coming Stopped by Hysterical Nun"). The capital letters and content make the sense clear to the actor, who will select an appropriate reading.

Contractions and Incomplete Sentences

Theatrical dialogue uses contractions to capture the sound of real-life people speaking naturally. Look back at the Cliff-Ralph scene and imagine the characters saying "I am" instead of "I'm," "let us" instead of "let's," "I have not seen you" instead of "haven't seen" or "did you not" instead of "didn't you." The result of such changes would be stilted dialogue at best, so ill-suited for the characters that they would be emasculated. Only the most formal characters in your play will say "cannot," "do not," or "I will," and such construction alone won't create a formal quality in the character.

Similarly, incomplete sentences, phrases, and elliptical construction often create effective dialogue. Few characters form spo-

ken sentences with the same attention to grammatical rules as
would a skilled writer.

Interruptions that Enliven Characterization

Humans seldom politely wait for the other person to finish a
thought. More frequently they interrupt each other. Those interruptions increase with the depth of emotional involvement. As
your characters become angry and upset, or delighted and over-
joyed, you'll find that they want to interrupt or override each other,
and the result is scenes that crackle with tension and excitement.
Note the interruptions that show the characters' emotional turmoil in the following example from Tennessee Williams's *The Glass
Menagerie*:

TOM: What in Christ's name am I—
AMANDA: *(Shrilly)* Don't you use that—
TOM: Supposed to do!
AMANDA: Expression! Not in my—
TOM: Ohhh!
AMANDA: Presence! Have you gone out of your senses?
TOM: I have, that's true, *driven* out!
AMANDA: What is the matter with you, you—big—big—IDIOT!
TOM: Look!—I've got *no thing*, no single thing—
AMANDA: Lower your voice!
TOM: In my life here that I can call my OWN! Everything is—
AMANDA: Stop that shouting!

Physical Action to Eliminate Words

A lively sense of theatre means, among other things, being alert
to the physical contributions the actors can make to express unspoken dialogue. In simplest terms, you can use actor directions
to replace dialogue with physical action. Instead of writing a line
that says, "Yes, I agree with you," you write the actor direction
(Nodding) and let the actor communicate the information. "Do you
want a drink from this bottle?" can become *(Holding bottle up and
looking inquiringly at him)*.

Consider John Pielmeier's use of an actor direction to replace
words in *Agnes of God*. In the following passage, Mother Miriam
Ruth is explaining to Dr. Livingstone how Agnes could conceal
her pregnancy from others in the convent:

DOCTOR: How did she hide it from the other nuns?
MOTHER: She undressed alone, she bathed alone.
DOCTOR: Is that normal?
MOTHER: Yes.
DOCTOR: How did she hide it during the day?
MOTHER: *(Shaking her habit)* She could have hidden a machine
gun in here if she had wanted.

Pielmeier might have given the Mother a lengthy explanation
such as "All of us nuns wear large, voluminous habits that can
hide most anything you can imagine," but it would have been less
effective than "shaking her habit." The simple actor direction
neatly eliminates excess words and uses the stage. Perhaps more
important to the playwright, actor directions are part of imaginatively *seeing* characters in action while writing the play, thus
helping bring them to life.

Variety and Contrast

Variety and contrast are important tools in many aspects of playwriting, and certainly in writing dialogue. Theatrical dialogue is
enlivened by variety in length of sentences and speeches, phrasing
or structure, word choice, imagery, use of incomplete phrases,
ellipses, and the like. Variation also creates contrast for emphasis:
A series of short speeches before a long speech will make the latter
stronger, and crude or mundane language emphasizes flights of
poetry.

Tmesis

Certain characters may be made vivid by tmesis, their way of
splitting a word or compound phrase by an expression put between
its parts, such as "absofuckinglutely" or "neverthehelllless." Because it draws attention to itself, use such a device judiciously and
sparingly; and because it is so distinctive, you'd likely give that
technique to only one character.

PRINCIPLES OF STRUCTURAL EMPHASIS

A sentence has three areas of strength: the end, which is the strongest; the beginning, second in strength; and the middle, the weakest
part of the sentence. The premise of structural emphasis is that

the most significant concept, word, phrase, or idea is placed at the end of the sentence, the secondary concept is placed at the beginning of the sentence, and the least important materials belong in the middle. Not all materials deserve emphasis. Use phrases for the least significant matters, clauses for moderately important ideas, and sentences for vital concepts.

Emphasis by Structure: The End of the Sentence

An old vaudevillian joke illustrates the concept that the most emphatic emphasis is at the end of the sentence.

STRAIGHT MAN: Who was that lady I saw you with last night?
COMIC: That was my wife, not a lady.

It just doesn't work. The comic punch belongs at the end of the sentence: "That was no lady: that was my wife."

Several speeches between Amanda and Tom in *The Glass Menagerie* illustrate theatrical dialogue that uses the emphatic ending position. The following example contains two incorrect uses of emphasis at the end of the speech.

(1) TOM: I thought perhaps a gentleman caller is what you wanted.
(2) TOM: A gentleman caller is what you wanted, I thought.
(3) TOM: I thought perhaps you wished for a gentleman caller.

The first two examples (which Williams did not write) are poorly written because they don't use emphasis correctly. The two key words—gentleman caller—for this sentence and for the play receive special attention because they are at the end of the sentence in the third example (which Williams wrote).

To illustrate emphasis in a longer sentence, examine Amanda's speech to Tom:

AMANDA: You are the only young man that I know of who ignores the fact that the future becomes the present, the present the past, and the past turns into everlasting regret if you don't plan for it!

The operative concept is "planning for the future," a key to Amanda's character throughout the play. The location at the end of the sentence gives the phrase strength.

Emphasis at the End of a Speech

As indicated above, the end of a sentence conveys the most emphasis. So, too, does the end of a speech. For illustration, note Lady Macbeth's "sleepwalking" speech (*Macbeth*, Act V, scene 1):

LADY MACBETH: Out, damned spot. Out, I say! One; two. Why then 'tis time to do't. Yet who would have thought there'd be so much blood in the old man? Hell is murky. Fie, my lord, fie! a soldier, and afeard? What need we fear who knows it, when none can call our power to account?

But that is not the way Shakespeare constructed the speech to build to a climax. The above speech is confused, muddy, and anticlimactic. This is the way Shakespeare used the climactic power of a speech's ending:

LADY MACBETH: Out, damned spot! Out, I say! One; two. Why then 'tis time to do't. Hell is murky. Fie, my lord, fie! a soldier, and afeard? What need we fear who knows it, when none can call our power to account? Yet who would have thought the old man to have had so much blood in him?

Note the differences in the two constructions of the final sentence. "Yet who would have thought there'd be so much blood in the old man?" "Yet who would have thought the old man to have had so much blood in him?" Moving "blood" closer to the end of the speech makes the second example stronger.

Emphasis by Structure: The Beginning of the Sentence

The discussion above indicates that sentence structure can create emphasis, and concludes that the most emphatic is the ending. Second in power is the sentence's beginning. In *Death of a Salesman*, for example, Arthur Miller gives Willy a sentence that places the emphasis on the beginning: "Chevrolet, Linda, is the greatest car ever built." (It would have been less effective if written this way: "Linda, I say a Chevrolet is the greatest car ever built.")

Later Willy says, " 'Cause I get so lonely—especially when business is bad and there's nobody to talk to." (The emphasis on "lonely" would have been lost if stuck in the middle of the sentence: "When business is bad I get lonely when there's nobody to talk to.")

Placement of Proper Names in Sentences and Questions

The principle of structural emphasis also affects placement of names in sentences. If at the end of the sentence, it may cause the actor to give little energy to the speech. Read the following examples aloud to yourself and note how the sentence fades off in the first example.

> "Yes, I want to go, Jim."
> "Yes, Jim, I want to go."

Placement of names at the end of sentences tends to weaken the speech. The tendency is perhaps more audible with questions. Again, read these examples aloud:

> "Do you want to get out, Jim?"
> "Jim, do you want to get out?"

SPECIAL ASPECTS OF DIALOGUE: IMAGERY AND POETRY, MONOLOGUES AND SOLILOQUIES

The revolutionary newness of The Glass Menagerie . . . *was in its poetic lift, but an underlying hard dramatic structure was what earned the play its right to sing poetically. Poetry in the theatre is not, or at least ought not be, a cause but a consequence, and that structure of storytelling and character made this very private play available to anyone capable of feeling at all.*

—Arthur Miller

We associate poetic diction with dramatists such as Shakespeare and Molière as well as with contemporary playwrights such as Federico García Lorca, Maxwell Anderson, Christopher Fry, T. S. Eliot, and other writers who use rhythm and images to bring music and song to their dialogue. If you want that special elevated speech, think of poetic diction as being like musical theatre: Playwrights-composers give characters song only when mere prose will not suffice. Illustrative songs include "I Could Have Danced All Night" and "I've Grown Accustomed to Her Face" from *My Fair Lady*, and "Tradition" and "Far from the Home I Love" from *Fiddler on the Roof*.

Poetry serves much the same purposes and is used for much the same reasons. Poetic diction is effective when prose cannot express the characters' depth and range of feelings. If you want to create poetry, don't start with word choices and imagery. Think instead of characters of sufficient size who can speak in elevated language and have feelings and needs that demand poetic diction. Poetic diction begins with the situation and the characters. Sprinkling poetic language and symbols throughout the play is not a recipe for success.

Simplicity often is effective, as illustrated in the following passage from Tennessee Williams's *A Streetcar Named Desire*. Blanche hopes Mitch will provide her the safe refuge she desperately needs.

MITCH: *(Drawing her slowly into his arms)* You need somebody. And I need somebody, too. Could it be—you and me, Blanche?

> *(She stares at him vacantly for a moment. Then with a soft cry huddles in his embrace. She makes a sobbing effort to speak but the words won't come. He kisses her forehead and her eyes and finally her lips. The Polka tune fades out. Her breath is drawn and released in long, grateful sobs.)*

BLANCHE: Sometimes—there's God—so quickly!

Blanche's five simple words demonstrate the power of poetic diction to express characters' emotional flights. It would be jarring, however, if the playwright gave her a poetic quality only this one time. Early in the play Williams establishes Blanche's ability to speak in elevated diction, making this speech a logical part of her emotional qualities throughout the play.

Williams also uses contrast effectively. Mitch's diction is ungrammatical and clumsy, the opposite of Blanche's; and his proposal, while heartfelt, certainly is mundane enough. That contrast further emphasizes the power of Blanche's speech.

Imagery

Imagery is enhanced diction, a description that awakens the audience to a place, an idea, an action, a thing, or an experience. You may use figurative imagery to speak indirectly to the audience's imagination or literal imagery to speak directly to the audience's knowledge. Least effective in theatrical dialogue are allusions consisting of only a word or phrase; successful use of imagery in theatre requires you to sustain and develop the material.

Some playwrights construct an entire play around an image. *The Glass Menagerie*, for example, centers around Laura's collection of small glass animals, delicate pieces that represent Laura's personality and Amanda's dreams. Other playwrights may use an image once to drive home a particular idea. Jean-Paul Sartre's *No Exit* has a particularly terrifying image that begins the play. Garcin and the Valet are on stage.

GARCIN: *(Eyes the VALET suspiciously)* I thought as much. That's why there's something so beastly, so damn bad-mannered, in the way you stare at me. They're paralyzed.

VALET: What are you talking about?

GARCIN: Your eyelids. We move ours up and down. Blinking, we call it. It's like a small black shutter that clicks down and makes a break. Everything goes black; one's eyes are moistened. You can't imagine how restful, refreshing, it is. Four thousand little rests per hour. Four thousand little respites—just think! . . . So that's the idea. I'm to live without eyelids. Don't act the fool, you know what I mean. No eyelids, no sleep; it follows, doesn't it? I shall never sleep again. But then—how shall I endure my own company?

The Monologue

A monologue is one character's extended speech. Unlike the aside, the monologue is heard by other onstage characters, and you want to be certain they are motivated to let the speaker talk at length without interrupting him or her. The speaker also must have reasons—usually heightened emotional involvement with the topic or issue—to speak for so long. The monologue's effectiveness is proven in plays by modern playwrights such as Edward Albee *(The*

Zoo Story) and Lanford Wilson *(The Madness of Lady Bright, Ludlow Fair,* and others).

The Soliloquy

The soliloquy is similar to the monologue in that it is one character's speech showing deep feelings and thoughts. Distinctions between the two terms are blurred, but generally the soliloquy is spoken when no one else is onstage. Some theatre people reserve "soliloquy" for speeches that are more formally or poetically constructed than monologues; others seem to use "soliloquy" for classical plays and "monologues" for more modern works.

The soliloquy was popular in Elizabethan drama, best illustrated in Shakespearean plays such as *Hamlet* and *Macbeth*. It faded in the nineteenth century with the advent of realism, which rejected its artificiality; but in modern theatre it comes back to life in works of playwrights such as Eugene O'Neill, Thornton Wilder, and Samuel Beckett.

DANGERS TO AVOID

Errors can creep into dialogue, making it weak and ineffective. No list of dangerous pitfalls can apply to all playwrights and plays—what may be successful dialogue for one playwright can become a source of strength for another—but we can describe certain common dangers that you want to avoid.

Repetition

As we discussed earlier, the rule of three suggests repetition helps ensure communication to audiences, but in other instances repetition can become irritating and boring. Most dangerous are senseless repetitions of previous speeches, as indicated below:

MARK: Do you want to tell me what to do?
MIMSY: Why should I tell you what to do?
MARK: Give me a break—I need some help.
MIMSY: You need help? No way. I'm not going to help you.
MARK: Why won't you help me?
MIMSY: Help you? Look, it's not my job.
MARK: But it is your job. You're supposed to help me.

MIMSY: By telling you what to do?
MARK: Hey, you caught on!

Horrible, isn't it? That sort of repetition is valuable only if the playwright intends the audience to thoroughly dislike these two insipid characters or if the playwright is getting paid by the word. Otherwise, avoid senseless repetition which destroys the play's forward movement, makes the characters appear witless, and too easily can become a habitual way of writing. Tennessee Williams, so often a master of dialogue, falls into the repetitive trap in his *Period of Adjustment*—"What you're going through here is a period of adjustment"—and repeats the phrase so often that audiences shudder.

Past Tense

Drama is an art of the present, with a lively sense of future. Past-tense verbs can drag the play out of its present into the past and deny movement toward the future. The play's focus on the present and future calls for phrases such as "I'm doing it (now)" and "I'll do it (tomorrow)," but not "I did it (five years ago)."

If you find your dialogue contains past-tense verbs, think of them as red flags that warn of a focus on the past. A limited number of past-tense verbs are almost essential to allow characters to show the relevance of their past to their present and future action. A large number, however, indicates you should ask yourself if your play might be better if you transfer the action to the past.

Junk Words

"Oh," "well," and "yeah" are junk words with little nutritional value. Typically found at the beginning of speeches, such words more likely come from the playwright than the character. Perhaps writing such words may help you get characters to speak during your initial stages of constructing the play, but during the revision process you should look carefully at junk words to see if they can be deleted. Most can.

Clichés

Clichés lack originality, making them especially inappropriate in playwriting. Although you may deliberately give a particular character trite expressions to show his or her mundane thought processes, the device should be used sparingly and judiciously. (You don't want the audience to conclude the clichés personify the playwright!)

Long and Complex Sentences

"Bill, that tire will have to be changed now because tomorrow noon, I must tell you, despite any objections you may have (and I was told by Sally that you'll have many), is the deadline for filing that paper I told you about last month: the application for our marriage license, which will have to be approved by the board of health."

Whew! Try reading that aloud on one breath, making sense of it while also showing the speaker's emotional attitude. Tough job, isn't it? The sense is clear, more or less, to the reader's eye. But what about the listener's ear? And the actor's problem reading it? Yet that line actually appears in a play (charity suggests we let the author remain anonymous). Can the dialogue be revised? Certainly. Start by getting rid of the passive voice in the first, parenthetical, and last phrases. Then eliminate nonessential words and express the emotion simply. Perhaps your revision may read like this: "Damn it, Bill! Fix the tire and go apply for our marriage license. Now!"

Consider the actor. Actors approach long sentences with trepidation, concerned that breath and energy may fade before they get to the end. No specific number of words defines a long sentence, but as a general rule it is perhaps twelve or more words. Yet more worrisome for actors are complex or convoluted sentences that twist and turn like snakes, burying the essential meaning. The more phrases and inversions, the more difficulty the actors will experience; the more problems they have, the greater the likelihood they won't read the line as effectively as you'd wish.

Simple sentences. Note that most examples of effective theatrical dialogue in this chapter are simple, direct sentences. Actors' apprehensions do not necessarily argue for a play containing only short sentences, which could become boring for the playwright to write, the actor to speak, and the audience to hear, but you do need to think of the actors' problems as you construct dialogue. Here is yet another reason you should read your play aloud, revising sentences that create problems for performers.

Long Speeches

Related to long sentences are long speeches, a common flaw in many plays. There are no guidelines suggesting that, say, three to four sentences per speech are acceptable but more than five fall into dangerous territory, but your writer's ear helps you recognize that long speeches can become windy, slow the play's pace, or exist for the playwright's convenience and not the characters' needs. One fears that often a speech is long simply because the playwright didn't cut and revise.

In special cases, however, long speeches can be powerful if the character is highly motivated. For example, "The Story of Jerry and the Dog" from Edward Albee's *Zoo Story* is a brilliant *tour de force*; and Blanche's speech about the deaths at Belle Reve is an emotional outburst that fits the play and character. The key is character motivation and emotion. Long speeches, we might conclude, are effective when used with restraint and then only if the character is compelled to speak at length.

Ask yourself the following six questions when you've written speeches over three or four sentences long:

- Do other characters want to interrupt? If so, give them opportunity to express their emotions, developing their characters. If they remain silent, their characterization is weakened.
- Does the long speech express a single idea, or are there several ideas uncomfortably shoved together? (Look out for phrases such as "and furthermore.") A good rule of thumb is for one speech to contain only one idea; a second idea is better expressed in a second speech.
- Is the character emotionally motivated to hold forth at length? If so, the long speech may be correct.
- Are there many long speeches throughout the play? Ask yourself if the play's pace suffers.
- Do the long speeches contain exposition, playwright's explanations, or other information that is better shown in action? If so, force yourself to revise the speeches.
- Are the long speeches evidence that the playwright is not disciplined? Are the speeches a writer's self-indulgence? If so, the remedy should be evident.

WORKING WITH ACTORS AND DIRECTORS

Your collaborators in art are the theatrical directors, actors, and designers who bring your play to life in a process that directors call "transferring the play from the page to the stage." As directors and actors will tell you, dialogue must be *stageworthy*, appropriate for theatre's unique requirements: You combine the craft of writing with the craft of oral speech aimed at the listener.

Focus on dialogue should not make us forget that theatre is an intensely visual medium, especially today. Modern audiences speak of going to *see* a play, in contrast to the Elizabethans who are described as "an assemblage of ears" because they went to *hear* a play. You therefore think of dialogue accompanying what the actors *do*.

Stage Directions

Stage directions (as differentiated from *actor directions*, explained below) allow the playwright to speak directly to those involved in the production—actors and designers of scenery, lighting, costumes, and sound—but primarily to the play's director, who has the responsibility of artistic unification of all effects. You use stage directions to communicate your vision of the environment, characters' mannerisms and physical appearance, various special effects involving lights and sound, and activity on the stage.

Actor Directions

Actor directions tell each actor how you heard the line, whether a laugh punctuates the speech, and so forth. These directions are aimed at the individual actor, in contrast to stage directions, which are designed for all involved in the production. For example, note George Bernard Shaw's use of actor directions in *Candida*, a play about a woman's choice between her husband, Reverend James Morrell, and a young poet, Eugene Marchbanks, who also loves her. (We should add that spelling and punctuation are Shaw's.)

CANDIDA: *(Slowly recoiling a step, her heart hardened by his rhetoric in spite of the sincere feeling behind it)* Oh! I am to choose am I? I suppose it is quite settled that I must belong to one or the other.

MORRELL: *(Firmly)* Quite. You must choose definitely.

MARCHBANKS: *(Anxiously)* Morrell: you dont understand. She means that she belongs to herself.

CANDIDA: *(Turning to him)* I mean that, and a good deal more, Master Eugene, as you will both find out presently. And pray, my lords and masters, what have you to offer for my choice? I am up for auction, it seems. What do you bid, James?

MORRELL: *(Reproachfully)* Cand—*(He breaks down: his eyes and throat fill with tears: the orator becomes a wounded animal)* I cant speak—

Memorization

In the premiere production of Samuel Beckett's *Waiting for Godot* the actors had major memorization problems, apparently as lost in the words as Beckett's characters are in the universe. The play's repetitions are difficult to memorize and keep in order, and many similar lines make it all too easy for actors to mistake cues, leading them to leap forward or backward in the script. Neil Simon's *Brighton Beach Memoirs* has two relatively identical exchanges between the brothers, structurally similar enough to make actors start the first scene but slip into the second.

Your consideration of the actor's problems should lead you to be wary of repeating identical exchanges at various parts of the play because the stress of public performance may cause an actor to leap from one such part to a distant other. Dialogue that has a natural, logical, cause-effect flow is easier for the actor to memorize. Not unimportantly, it is easier for the audience to comprehend.

Offstage Dialogue

Offstage dialogue presents problems to actors and directors because audiences hear and comprehend speakers who are visible more easily than those who are invisible. Furthermore, actors may lose characterization if they must labor to make offstage dialogue audible through the muffling effect of scenery. Good theatre practice suggests that you use few, if any, offstage speeches. Those that are absolutely essential should be brief, easy to understand, and relatively unimportant to the plot or characterization.

Sibilants

A series of words that contain hissing sounds can become hurdles that trip actors. They won't enjoy the challenge you give them by carelessly writing phrases such as "his zeal is zero," and you won't enjoy listening to them slow down to get through the problem as they focus more on avoiding a hiss (or, more unfortunately, a whistle) and less on character and interpretation.

EXERCISES

1. Use the following as a springboard and write four to six pages of dialogue between these two characters.

    HEATHER: *(Quietly)* Is it time?
    SALLY JO: *(Looking nervously at the door)* Not yet.
    HEATHER: Don't be afraid.
    SALLY JO: But they said . . .
    HEATHER: Shhhh.

    When you've finished, check the dialogue to be certain you've (a) used the rule of three to establish the time, place, and action, (b) made each character's dialogue unique, (c) communicated each character's goal and emotions, (d) avoided overly long sentences or speeches, and (e) given the dialogue snap and crackle. Read through the dialogue to eliminate as many words as possible. Add actions to replace words.

2. Remove two major characters from the play you're writing, put them in a new situation, and repeat the first exercise. Write four to six pages of dialogue, then revise as necessary.

3. Examine ten pages of dialogue you have written and make the following changes, admittedly quite arbitrary but presented here for you to use as an experiment.

    Force yourself to delete at least ten to twenty words per page. Does that improve the dialogue?

    Find at least one place per page where you will substitute physical actions for words. Do you think that makes the dialogue more interesting?

    Revise at least two speeches per page so they do not contain grammatically correct sentences but instead are unfinished thoughts or phrases. Does that give the dialogue a better flow?

    Require at least two interruptions per page. What does that do to the characterization?

    Force yourself to increase the emotional tonality of several of the protagonist's speeches. Does that seem to improve the character?

4. Select any play you admire and copy (by hand or on a keyboard) a page of its dialogue. What do you learn about the flow of its dialogue? Then try to revise that page. Do you find places where revisions would be absolutely wrong? Or other places where revisions may help the dialogue? What qualities make the differences?

Howard Lindsay has said, and very rightly, that a couple of lines can make a scene too long, four lines make it very much too long, and six can make it impossible. You would not have thought that cutting four lines out of a scene can make much difference. I have done it, and I know it can. . . . Cutting, and a willingness to cut, are two things that can serve a playwright best. . . . Few plays have been damaged by cutting, and most have been improved. I am talking now of cutting not only lines, but words.

—John Van Druten

8

Evaluating and Revising Your Play

Come Blow Your Horn was eight weeks in the writing, three years in the rewriting, and it had at least eight producers before I ever saw it on a stage.

NEIL SIMON

Your play is finished!

Or is it?

Probably not. Although a self-congratulatory party certainly is in order to celebrate completing a draft of your play, now prepare yourself for the crucial next step: revisions. Experienced playwrights say "plays are not written but are rewritten" because revising your play is at least as important as writing it, and the revision process often makes the difference between a script that is performed onstage and one that never leaves the page.

Neil Simon, perhaps modern theatre's most frequently produced playwright, spent three years rewriting one of his highly successful plays. Simon's experience is not unusual. Eugene O'Neill's diary shows he worked five years rewriting and revising *Mourning Becomes Electra* from start to production version, and he expected more revisions when he heard the cast read the script. Arthur Miller spent two years revising *All My Sons*. Tennessee Williams wrote at least half a dozen drafts of his works before showing them to others; one started as a film script called *The Gentleman Caller* and went through numerous revisions over several years before it became *The Glass Menagerie.* Virtually every professional play-wright has similar stories about rewriting.

We hope it will not take you as many years to see your play staged. (You can shorten the process if you start with short mono-dramas or one-act plays instead of full-lengths, and aim at local theatres and workshops instead of Broadway.) Still, it is safe to conclude that if O'Neill, Simon, Williams, and Miller had to spend two or three years revising (and revising and revising) a play until it met their goals, other playwrights can expect that revisions will be a complicated process. You'll want to cultivate what we might call the "Three P's for Playwrights"—perseverance, patience, and persistence. Prepare yourself mentally and emotionally to rewrite your play, and allow ample time to do a thorough job.

You start by shifting mental gears from the creative mode to a careful analytical technique to evaluate your play. Your goal is to find your play's strengths, which you want to enhance, and its weaknesses, which you must correct. The revision process can be divided into three parts: accepting the idea that rewrites will im-prove your play, working alone in the privacy of your work space, and working with others.

THE REVISION PROCESS FOR ALL WRITERS

> *The most essential gift for a good writer is a built-in, shock-proof shit detector.*
>
> —Ernest Hemingway

The single most important component of an effective revision process can be stated simply for all writers: Accept the fact that revisions are essential. Never ignore rough, awkward, or incom-plete places in your script, thinking that they don't matter. They do.

You need to face a blunt truth: The playwright who refuses to revise has little chance of surviving theatre's realities. Rewriting simply comes with the writer's territory. Accepting that fact de-creases the difficulties that are caused by reluctance to revise.

Keep the First Draft to Yourself

All writers know that they should never show a first draft to any-one. The first version simply isn't ready for exposure, and the writer's pride in his or her craftsmanship forbids letting anyone see a manuscript with flaws. Think of the responses you'll receive if you do show that initial version to someone. Will that reader's comments be helpful? Probably not: The reader won't be able to overlook rough areas to find the essence of the play. Will the reader's responses be harmful? Quite possibly: Comments that focus on mistakes can damage the writer's morale. Think, too, of the reader who sees a flawed first draft: Will he or she be eager to see later versions? Not likely.

Despite your understandable delight that you've completed a draft of your play, before you share your play with others you must first be sure it says precisely what you want it to say, neither more nor less, and in exactly the way you want to say it. Vladimir Nabokov makes the point vividly: "Only ambitious nonentities and hearty mediocrities exhibit their rough drafts. It is like passing around samples of one's own sputum."

WORKING ALONE TO REVISE YOUR PLAY

For three years Painting Churches *was about a girl coming home and having her mother make a dress for her debut as a pianist. For three years I struggled and struggled, writing eight drafts which weren't bad, but they didn't work. Finally I got the idea that the girl would be a portrait painter and was coming home to paint her parents' portrait. It was a moment of blinding awareness, an epiphany. And everything fell together. That's how we playwrights work.*

—Tina Howe

Where do you start revising? How do you evaluate your script? What parts of the play should you examine? No one revision system can be correct for all playwrights, but a key to successful revisions involves a step-by-step method that will help you look at your script objectively. Here we discuss analytical approaches you may find effective.

Read the Play Aloud to Yourself

Your first step is to read your finished play aloud to yourself. The key is "aloud." A play is designed to be spoken aloud by actors, quite a different process from reading it silently to oneself like a novel. As you read, become the characters, imitate actors you'd like to perform the roles, stride around the room, shout the explosive lines, whisper the tender moments, and experience the emotions.

Try to avoid looking for minor changes at this point. You aren't worried about a sentence here or a speech there. Instead, look at the overall effect of the play and ask yourself questions. What do I want to say? Is the play's meaning clear? Does the play have a unifying thread, shown by the characters in action? Is the conflict real and genuine? Is there enough action? Does it need more complications? Does it take place in the present, moving toward a future? Are there slow scenes that ought to be changed? Are the scenes in the correct order? Do the scenes build, increasing tensions? As you listen to the play, mark the script's problem areas, then revise the script.

Read Aloud Individual Characters

After reading the entire play aloud, the next step is to check characterization by going through the full play and reading aloud only one character at a time. Start with the protagonist and then repeat the process with each other character. Are they all drawn as thoroughly and richly as you want? Does each respond appropriately to stimuli from other characters? Does each character evolve and change? Are the characters different from one another? Does each have individualistic dialogue and characteristics? Reading each character will help you revise the script. Repeat the process as many times as necessary until you cannot find areas to revise.

Put the Play Aside to Let It "Cool"

Playwrights often put their completed plays aside for a period of time, believing a cooling-off period allows them to return later with a more dispassionate objectivity that makes revisions easier. You may wish to experiment with this technique, but avoid letting the play sit so long that you lose interest in it.

WORKING WITH OTHERS TO REVISE YOUR PLAY

Put yourself in a position where you can get your plays made public. Not that they'll always be fully performed, but at least

*done in classes where they'll be read out loud. Go public as
soon as you can. Don't turn up your nose at coffeehouse
productions or high school readings. Get out there and get
it down. Don't harbor plays in your trunk; doing them whets
your appetite.*

—A. R. Gurney, Jr.

Theatre is a collaborative art that is based on sharing different talents to achieve a mutual goal. Working with actors and directors helps you revise your play, puts you in close contact with collaborators, and makes you think of your play as a stage piece. Your contacts with local community, regional, or educational theatres will help you find actors and directors who are willing to participate in developing a new play. Characteristic of the generous nature of many theatre artists, actors and directors often will be eager to contribute their talents.

Have Actors Read the Play to You

When you've finished revising the play as best you can, put the script in the hands of actors and ask them to read it aloud for you. Let the play stand on its own. Avoid directing the actors; don't tell them how to interpret the characters or the lines; evade their questions about the play or the characters. Instead, encourage actors to use their creative insight to show you what they see in the play and the characters. Mark the play for revisions as they read. Consider tape-recording the reading for future study in the privacy of your quiet work space.

Often the readings will help you find areas that need shortening. Christopher Durang, for example, said an early reading of his *Sister Mary Ignatius Explains It All for You* showed him ten minutes that "screamed out, 'Cut me. Cut me.'" At other times you may discover that your play has lost sight of its goal. Lillian Hellman said that quiet readings helped her refind the focus of *The Little Foxes*.

When the actors finish reading, invite their comments and questions, guiding them to speak primarily about characterization and dialogue, which they know well. Actors can give you insightful comments about character motivation, awkward or confusing dialogue, and even details about the characters' biography and history. Listen to critiques without interrupting them or becoming defensive. Take notes to show that you care about their observations. Look over the notes later when you are more objective. Revise the script, then ask the same or different actors to read the revised play again. Repeat the process until you cannot find revisions.

Improvisations Help Writing and Revising

As you work with actors and directors, ask them to help you explore aspects of your play with improvisational experiments (improvs), which are rehearsal techniques actors use to probe character and develop situations by going beyond the written dialogue and plot. Improvs can help you enrich and sustain scenes, add dimension to characterization, find areas that lack sufficient material, and see ways to substitute action for words. Well-guided improvs start with the script and depend on the actors already having a firm grip on characterization.

We can illustrate the value of improvisations with a small scene. Suppose, for example, you are writing a play that has two lovers who have been fighting. You plan for the male to leave. Your scene ends like this:

BETH: You can leave now.
DUFF: All right, damn it, I *will* go.
BETH: Good-bye.
DUFF: I . . . I—Oh, hell. *(He exits.)*

From the readings you may decide that the scene lacks richness. The characters' emotions are thin. Duff's exit seems rushed. The scene needs to be sustained and amplified. You can get the actors' insight in the scene by asking them to improvise how they feel, using physical activities as well as words. They may show you something like this:

BETH: You can leave now.
DUFF: All right. . . . *(He starts toward the door, pauses, looks back at her, waiting for her to speak. She doesn't.)* Damn it, I *will* go. *(He doesn't move.)* Beth . . . ?
BETH: Good-bye.
DUFF: *(He marches to the door, stops again, not looking at her.)* Is that all you can say—just good-bye?

BETH: Look, buddy, you've used me for the last time. I'm sick of you.

DUFF: Damn it!

BETH: Good-bye.

Perhaps the director says Beth's lines about being "used" is awkward and not powerful enough to motivate Duff to leave. Ask the actress not to use the speech you wrote. Possibly she'll improvise an action similar to this:

DUFF: Is that all you can say—just good-bye?

BETH: *(She purses her lips to kiss him from the distance, then smiles at him, a big, radiant, artificially bright smile.)* See ya, sailor.

DUFF: Go to hell. *(He exits.)*

Here we looked at only a few lines in a short scene. Expand on this single example to use improvs to help you with longer scenes that appear wrong.

Ask a Trusted Theatre Expert to Critique the Script

By now you have revised the play perhaps five to ten times and are ready to ask for a detailed critique from a theatre expert such as a playwriting teacher, a director, an educational theatre professor, another playwright, or an actor. Persistence may be necessary because such people often are reluctant to critique something as personal as a playwright's work and some may not want to expend the rather large amount of time necessary for a thorough critique. You may be able to overcome their reservations by telling them what you've done to revise the play to this point and showing them that you will respect their comments. Let those insights help you revise the script again.

Evaluate the Evaluations

Expect actors, directors, and playwriting experts to give you more suggestions than you can use. Some actors and directors get so involved with critiquing an original play that it becomes like a popular sport that unfortunately lacks viable rules. Evaluate the evaluations. Start by listening dutifully to the comments. Avoid becoming argumentative but mentally reserve the right to accept or reject comments according to their value to you and your play.

Some comments will seem more "here's the play I wish you'd write" and less "here's a response to the play you wrote." Those are easily rejected. Better critiques contain specific information and suggestions that will help you revise your play. Listen imaginatively and focus on what the critic is attempting to say but unable to put into words. Pay special attention to areas that bother several critics.

Ultimately, however, this is *your* play, and only you can decide what changes to make. You may even echo George Bernard Shaw's truculent rejection of comments:

> I am quite familiar with the fact that every fool who is connected with a theatre, from the call boy to the manager, thinks he knows better than an author how to make a play popular and successful. Tell them, with my compliments, that I know all about that, that I know my business and theirs as well.

(Or perhaps you ought to delay quoting Shaw until you achieve a reputation similar to his.)

"Script-in-Hand" Reading

You'll learn a great deal about your play from a script-in-hand reading, which is presented without production values such as scenery or lighting but with well-cast and rehearsed actors and performed for a small audience. Carrying the script allows the actors to focus on characterization and dialogue; because they have scripts, you are free to revise up to the last minute without worrying if they have time to memorize new material. If the play is presented on several nights, audience reaction can show you areas to revise. Test the new material in front of a new audience.

Workshop Productions

Slightly more advanced than script-in-hand readings, workshop productions may be simple or complex. Actors will have memorized their roles, and a director will have rehearsed them to achieve the play's values. Production values usually are limited; seldom will there be scenery or costumes other than what the actors can supply from personal wardrobes, and lighting may be simple illumination. The lack of production values places more focus on the play itself, and audience response will be enlightening. You'll find more areas to revise.

Who Will Give Your Play a Showing?

Locating organizations willing to do script-in-hand or workshop productions of your play is difficult but not impossible. Chapter 10, Resources for the Playwright, tells how to find them. In metropolitan areas you'll find a number of theatres and organizations that regularly present workshop or showcase productions, exemplified by Manhattan's off-off Broadway workshop theatres. In smaller towns turn to educational, community, or dinner theatres. If you work in a local theatre, you ought to be able to recruit actors and a director, and together you can convince management to set aside an evening for a small production. You can always form your own group of playwrights and actors, perhaps meeting at someone's home or using local library or church facilities.

A CHECKLIST OF QUESTIONS TO CONSIDER AT EACH STEP OF REVISION

> *Ultimately, the script has to answer the questions the actors have. If the answer is not in the script, then something has to be done. Rewriting* Mass Appeal *was educational. I learned a lot about writing, getting the point down to the bone, making the line as spare and right as possible.*
> —Bill C. Davis

"Every book, director, and playwright tells me that I'm supposed to revise," said a playwright at a national theatre workshop. "It's frustrating to be told that repeatedly but never be told *what* I should look for in my play. How do I know what to revise?" Other playwrights at the meeting agreed. The complaint is valid.

Here we list basic questions to help you evaluate your play. Use the questions selectively—not all will pertain to your particular play—and let this checklist help you create additional questions.

THE PLAY'S OVERALL EFFECT

These questions deal with the "feel" of your play, the overall impression it creates.

The Playwright's Goal

- What do I want to say? Where does the play achieve that goal, and where does it miss?
- Is the play true to itself? Does it achieve what it sets out to do?
- Does the play's intensity show that it represents something deeply important to me?
- Is the play's action plausible, possible, and probable?
- Is the play credible? Do characters have motivations for their actions, or are they obviously the playwright's puppets?
- Does the play have intrigue? Does it make the audience want to know what will happen next?
- Does the play have a sense of urgency that forces action to happen now, not yesterday or tomorrow?
- Is the action set in the present, not the past?
- Does the play have a sense of future?
- Is there enough surprise in the play?
- Is the play theatrical, requiring production to come to life?
- Is it compressed, or does it seem overextended? Should scenes be cut? Enlarged?
- Does the play exploit dramatic situations?
- Do the pieces of the play fit together seamlessly so the machinery doesn't show?

The Play's Intellectual Core

What does your play mean? What is the intellectual core, the sum of all action and character movement? These questions help you discover if your play communicates the desired meaning.

- Does the play's title imply something important about the play's meaning? Is the title subtle yet evocative?
- Does the protagonist's goal aid the audience in perceiving the play's meaning?
- Is a major dramatic question established at the point of attack and concluded at the climax? Does that question reflect significant aspects of the play's meaning?
- Does the total action of the play add up to indicate the play's intellectual core?
- Does the play's conflict suggest the play's meaning?
- Is there a linkage between inciting incident, point of attack,

protagonist's goal and plan, conflict, and climax? Do these pieces fit together? Should they be clarified or made more subtle?
- Have you avoided a curtain speech that speaks directly to the play's meaning?

CHARACTERIZATION

The following questions deal with your play's characterization. Three categories help you focus on the protagonist, antagonist, and all characters.

The Protagonist

- Do I intend my play to have a protagonist? If so, does the action make clear who is the protagonist?
- Does he or she appear early in the play?
- Is the protagonist directly involved with the point of attack?
- Does the protagonist have a visible, dominant, active goal?
- Is the protagonist strongly motivated to pursue the goal?
- Is the goal deeply important to the protagonist?
- Is that goal clear to the audience?
- Do actions make clear what he or she wants?
- Does the character have emotional and intellectual involvement with his or her goal?
- Does the protagonist have a plan to achieve the goal?
- Is that plan clear to the audience?
- Does he or she respond appropriately and dynamically to obstacles, reversals, and setbacks?
- Do I want the audience to like the protagonist? To respect him or her? If so, have I achieved my goal?
- Is the protagonist's goal one that the audience will approve?

The Antagonist

- If I have a protagonist, is there an opposing force?
- Is the antagonist clear to the audience?
- Does the antagonist have visible, clear, strong reasons to oppose the protagonist?
- Is the antagonist's goal clear?

- Does the antagonist take enough action to oppose the protagonist?
- Is the antagonist-protagonist relationship clear to the audience?

All Characters

- Do the characters (at least the primary characters) change and evolve during the play? Are the characters different because of the action they've undergone?
- Are the characters interesting? Can they be made more compelling?
- Are all characters essential to the play? Can one or more be eliminated? Will the play be tighter if I combine several characters into one?
- Do the characters have emotions? Are those strong, primary emotions? Are they clear to the audience?
- Are the characters different from one another? If they are similar, can contrasts give them added dimension and increase the tension and action of the play?
- Does each character have motivation for what he or she says and doesn't say, does and doesn't do?
- Does each *care* about what he or she is doing and saying?
- Do I want the audience to like one or more characters? Dislike specific ones? Does my play achieve that goal?
- Does each character have a reaction appropriate to each stimulus?
- Do the characters appear to have a life outside the universe of the play? Do they exist only for the play's structure, or do they have a life that goes beyond the play's walls?
- Are there thankless roles, such as purely utilitarian characters? If so, are they genuinely essential to the play or should they be eliminated?
- Does each character want to say each speech and do every action? Or do they appear to say or do things merely for the playwright's convenience?

DIALOGUE

Dialogue often is the most noticeable element of your play. The following questions direct your attention to aspects of dialogue.

- What can I delete? Can I substitute one word for four?
- Is the dialogue colorful, containing images, figures of speech, elliptical phrases, interruptions, active verbs?
- Does the dialogue have enough variety? Are there variations in length of speeches?
- Is the dialogue speakable?
- Does it come from the character?
- Is the dialogue theatrical (that is, a selected and artistic reproduction of these particular characters' speech), or is it literary (that is, designed less to be spoken and more to be read silently like an essay or novel)?
- Is the dialogue constructed with active, present-tense verbs? Can I change past-tense references to present action?
- Does each character have his or her unique speech patterns?
- Is each character's speech his or her own, or do they all speak with the playwright's tongue?
- Are long speeches (say, more than three or four sentences) essential?
- During long speeches, are there stimuli that should make other characters speak? Should they break in to express their reactions?
- Do long speeches reveal character, promote plot movement, and come from the character's driving need to speak at such length?
- Are sentences too long for the actor to handle? Can such sentences be shortened?
- Does the dialogue flow easily from the actors' mouths? Are there words or lines that make the actors stumble?
- Does the play contain dialogue that seems to indicate the playwright wants to be viewed as intellectual or well read? If so, can those speeches be revised or eliminated?
- Do speeches start with junk words, such as "well" and "oh"? If so, can I delete such words?
- Do speeches suffer from repetitive or rephrasing statements that merely echo what another character just said?

PLOT

A play's structure often is difficult to analyze because character and dialogue capture one's attention. The following questions help you focus on the structure of your play's action.

- Is there conflict? Is it clear? Is it sustained?
- Does the structural action of the play enhance, emphasize, show, and reflect the play's overall meaning?
- Does the play have a beginning, middle, and end? Is each adequately developed? Do the three have a clear interrelationship?
- Does the play start with mood-setting? Can that be eliminated or reduced?
- Is the inciting incident clear? Is it linked to the point of attack?
- Is exposition heavy-handed? Is one character forced to deliver exposition in large chunks? Does the character *need* to say an exposition speech? Can you delete it or make it more subtle? Can exposition be delayed until later in the play?
- Does foreshadowing draw the audience's attention to future action?
- Can I revise the play so it starts *in medias res*? Would starting in the midst of things improve the play's dramatic tension?
- Would the play be improved with an earlier point of attack?
- Does the point of attack change the course of action?
- Is the point of attack adequately sustained?
- Does the point of attack stimulate characters (especially the protagonist) into action?
- Does the point of attack pose the play's major dramatic question? Is the MDQ (major dramatic question) clear?
- Is the point of attack followed by another complication that reflects and enhances the beginning of the action?
- Are there enough complications, obstacles, reversals, and discoveries? Is each adequately sustained and developed?
- Do entrances and exits create complications? Do they change the course of action?
- Are entrances and exits sustained and exploited?
- Do entrances and exits defuse ongoing conflict? Should the characters stay on stage longer to enhance the action?
- Does the play's overall action make the play grow?
- Is the climax linked to the point of attack?
- Does the climax answer the play's major dramatic question? Is the answer clear?
- Does the play end? Or merely stop?

THE PLAY'S BEGINNING, MIDDLE, AND END

Often you can get a strong concept of your play's effect by thinking of its beginning, middle, and end as separate parts.

The Beginning

- Is the play's beginning compelling? Is it interesting? Will it make audiences want to see the rest of the play?
- Does the tone of the beginning indicate if the play will be comic or dramatic?
- Will the audience know each character's name?
- Do the characters immediately show a distinguishing quality that makes them easy to remember?
- Do I use the rule of three to repeat vital information three times to ensure clear communication to the audience?
- Is the play's inciting incident clear?
- Is exposition subtle?
- Does the point of attack have sufficient impact? Is it adequately sustained? Does it clearly change the play's course of action? Does it change the existing sense of equilibrium?
- Does the opening help the audience understand possible directions the action make take?
- Am I satisfied that the play's protagonist has a goal that the audience can recognize?

The Middle

- Is the play's protagonist forced to struggle to achieve his or her objective?
- Does the protagonist have sufficient struggles?
- Count the number of complications (reversals, obstacles). Am I satisfied there are neither too many nor too few?
- Do entrances and exits add to the action?
- Is each complication adequately sustained?
- Does each complication change the course of the play's action?
- Are the complications all part of a master action?
- Does the middle contain surprises that are nonetheless appropriate?
- Do the characters change and evolve during the action?

The End

- Does the ending coincide with showing the outcome of the protagonist's goal?
- Does the ending supply an answer to the major dramatic question? Is that answer clear? Does the answer link to the protagonist's goal?
- Am I certain that the play has only one climax?
- Is the play's climax appropriately sized to the struggle, neither too small nor too large?
- Have I avoided *deus ex machina* devices to end the play?
- Have I avoided an O. Henry ending?

DESIRED AUDIENCE RESPONSE

Playwrights face a number of paradoxes. One is the dichotomy of intent: On one hand, you write the play to please yourself, but on the other, your play should be aimed at a particular audience. Here you ask questions designed to help you consider audience response.

- For whom is my play written? Describe the ideal audience, thinking of age, education, level of sophistication, and the like. Examine the play through that audience's eyes. Do you find areas to change?
- What theatre do I have in mind? Is the play intended for college theatres? High schools? Community theatres? Broadway? Religious institutions? Does my play appeal to that theatre?
- If an excellent critic I respect saw a production of my play, what review would I hope to get? Does my play measure up to that review? What should I revise to be sure a critic will respond as I want?
- What is the desired audience response? State it briefly, clearly, and without fence-straddling or other equivocations that the play is all things to all people. Does the play achieve my intended response?
- What can I revise to achieve that desired audience response? Do all aspects of the play combine to create that response? Are any counterproductive? If so, can I eliminate them?
- Do I intend the audience to see my play as a comedy? Drama?

Where in particular does my play achieve that response? Where does it miss its target?

• Will the play offend the sensibilities of some audience members? Does that bother me?

The writer's intention hasn't anything to do with what he achieves. The intent to earn money or the intent to be famous or the intent to be great doesn't matter at the end. Just what comes out.

—Lillian Hellman

9

Script Format: Typing Your Script for Producers and Directors

Knowing that playwrights must live with a number of rules, you won't be surprised to encounter dictatorial statements regarding the typographical format of your playscript. Here we describe general and specific requirements to help you prepare your play to mail or give to theatrical producers, directors, agents, or publishers. Although you may feel that some typographical rules are arbitrary and busywork (and yes, they are), they are the standards by which your script is judged. Live with them until you have established your reputation as a produced playwright, then break them as you wish.

GENERAL GUIDELINES

You want your typed play to show a professional's care and pride in workmanship: If the play's overall physical appearance looks professional, you've started convincing readers that the play itself is excellent. Therefore you'll want to use professional writers' standards. These guidelines are relatively common for all writers.

Typing Your Play

Paper. Type your script, using only one side of 8½ x 11 paper. Never use the "easy erase" paper, which has an irritating way of smudging itself or leaving stains on shirt sleeves. Most likely you

170

will mail photocopies of your play; ordinary quality photocopy paper is acceptable, but you may want to use heavier grade (and more expensive) bond for special recipients.

Typeface. Use *pica* size type, not *elite*. Although you may have a word processing program and printer that can create a number of typefaces and fonts, avoid the temptation: One typeface is sufficient. If you're determined to take advantage of the printer's bells and whistles, you might use special fonts for the title and preliminary pages but not the script itself. Avoid, too, the temptation to use your program's ability to justify the right margin.

Margins. Your goal is a script that appeals to the eye: Use white space so the pages won't be full of dark type. Although you can vary the margins, a good guideline is to allow one inch for the top and right margins and one to one and one-half inches for the bottom margin. The left margin should be about one and one-half inches to permit binding. If you use pica type, these margins will give you approximately 62 spaces horizontally for dialogue.

Binding. Create a positive first impression with an attractive binder. Professional typing and photocopying services supply binders and will even emboss the title and your name on the front cover, but your local stationery store will have perfectly adequate (and less expensive) materials.

Spelling and Grammatical Errors

Proofread your script carefully and repeatedly to correct all errors before you give it to anyone. Spelling and grammatical errors are not acceptable. The second or third misspelled word in your script gives readers the right to conclude you have no pride in your craft, and they may return your play unread. Play readers such as producers' assistants, agents, and contest judges, who must evaluate hundreds of plays in a brief time, face the uncomfortable responsibility of finding reasons to reject plays. Errors in spelling, grammar, or script format give them sufficient reason. Furthermore, errors signal a careless writer, and experienced readers know that someone who is careless in writing may be unreliable in other ways as well.

Exceptions. The only exceptions to this rule are deliberate misspellings, such as when you write dialect or indicate a character's individualistic way of pronouncing words (for example, "I ain't gonna do it" or "I'm jist a-sittin' 'n' a-thinkin' 'bout it"). You can violate grammatical rules within dialogue (but not elsewhere), providing incorrect grammar depicts the character.

SPECIFIC GUIDELINES FOR THE PLAYSCRIPT

We can always hope that a great play will be recognized regardless of its typed form, but you must remember that your play is one of literally hundreds submitted to producers, directors, and agents. No playwright wants to risk rejection simply because the script isn't typed correctly. Here we discuss specific elements of proper form, then use sample pages from a play to illustrate the application of typographical format (see pages 177–184).

Basic Reasons for Script Format

Understanding the rationale for a particular playscript format will help you apply the system to your play. The following reasons underlie the standard form.

- Your typed script is intended for producers, directors, designers, and actors who will bring your play to life on stage, and therefore you use the typographical form that they prefer. For example, the standard script format allows estimation of the play's playing time (one typed page roughly equals one minute of time on stage), and other typographical devices help production personnel quickly find information they need.
- Ignore the formats you see in play anthologies, because those publications are designed for readers, not production personnel. The publishers' printed style is designed to save paper and printing expenses, not to help those involved in the staging process.
- Tradition is important (although not necessarily always good), and professional theatre workers expect playwrights to use the standard typographical style that they've learned to believe is best. Some believe that a play typed in any other format suggests that the playwright lacks a basic knowledge of theatre, leading them to doubt the value of the play itself.

PRELIMINARY PAGES

The preliminary pages consist of title page and the page(s) for cast of characters, time, and place. These are not numbered.

Title Page

The first page gives the play's title, centered and in all capital letters and underlined, plus a brief statement about the length (that is, A One-Act Play or A Three-Act Play). The author's name, also centered, is under the title. At the bottom of the page indicate copyright information (on the left side of the page) and author's mailing address and phone number (on the right side).

Cast, Time, and Place

The second page lists Cast of Characters (names, brief descriptions, and relationships if pertinent) and short statements about the Time and Place. Each of these three titles is typed in all capital letters, underlined, and centered. For a multi-act or -scene play, describe time and place for each act or scene.

Pagination

Page numbers are placed in the upper right-hand corner of each page. Some playwrights also include a key word from the title. Page count begins with the first page of the actual script, not counting preliminary pages such as title or cast pages.

Pagination for full-length plays. A full-length play or multi-scene play uses a combination of Roman and Arabic numerals to indicate act, scene, and page. For example, correct identification of the first act, first scene, and third page would read: I-1-3. I-2-15 indicates first act, second scene, fifteenth page; II-1-52 indicates second act, first scene, and fifty-second page. Note that the final number (52 in the last example) always is the total number of pages; don't start recounting with each new act or scene. If your play has only one scene in the act, omit the middle number (that is, II-52).

Pagination for one-act plays. For a one-act play you simply number each page consecutively without Roman numerals. A one-act play with more than one scene, however, requires the same system as a full-length. I-1-20 indicates the act, first scene, and twentieth page; I-2-21 indicates the act, second scene, and twenty-first page.

The typist finds that this pagination system quickly becomes a boring chore because it demands typing the digits on each page, and you must redo the numbers when you add or delete materials as you revise. If you're lucky, you have a computer with a word processing program that can handle the multiple-digit entries. One solution is to ignore all digits except the page number while you're writing various drafts of your script, inserting the full, hyphenated pagination only when you are preparing a final, smooth copy.

THE SCRIPT ITSELF

Please be patient here: Describing the script's typographical style makes the process appear more complicated than it actually is in practice. You need to learn how to use only three basic devices: indentation, line spacing (double versus single), and capitalization (all capital letters versus capital and lowercase).

An Invisible Middle Vertical Line

Imagine an invisible line that runs vertically down the page, somewhat to the left of the center. If your horizontal typing area is approximately sixty-two spaces, left to right, the vertical line is indented twenty-six spaces. That line is the left margin for stage directions and character names.

Stage Directions

Identation. Stage directions are the playwright's communication to directors, actors, designers, and technical personnel, such as for lighting and sound. They are indented to the vertical line described above (approximately twenty-six spaces from the left margin), placed in the right half of the page. Stage directions are single-spaced. Contrary to typed scripts you may see, stage directions are never enclosed in parentheses: The indentation is sufficient to set them off from the dialogue.

Capital letters for special effects. Use all capital letters to call attention to special design effects, such as lights and sound. For example, if you want the play to take place in shadows and there's a loud explosion offstage, you'd start with LIGHTS and SOUND, in all capital letters, and then describe the effect:

> LIGHTS: It is dim, shadowy, with little light through the window. SOUND: A loud explosion, like a shotgun, offstage in the front yard.

Don't use "Stage left" or "Stage right." Note that the above stage direction specifies the location of the explosion (in the front yard), but does not say "offstage right" or "offstage left." Never write "left," "right," "center," or other terms referring to the stage's geographical area, because that infringes on the responsibilities of directors and designers. They, not the playwright, decide what's stage left and right. They design the set according to their needs, artistic vision, theatre's architecture, and budget. What you referred to as "left" can become "right," making your stage directions confusing. Your job is to say where it happens in the play's world, not on the theatre's stage. It's fine for you to use stage directions to say a character "walks to the window," but it's incorrect to write that he "walks to the down left window."

Similarly, use all capital letters whenever you write instructions to actors describing what they're doing or wearing and the like. Capital letters draw the actor's attention to that material:

> SMITH jumps under the bed when he hears the explosion. Then HE yells and jumps back up, mumbling, shaking his head. SMITH'S fingers are in a mousetrap. HE manages to get free and puts HIS fingers in HIS mouth.

Characters' Names to Identify Speakers

Identation and spacing. Identify speakers by typing characters' names before their dialogue. Indent approximately twenty-six spaces to that same vertical line margin (which is not the same thing as centering each name). Type the speaker's name in all capital letters. A double space separates each name from the preceding material, whether dialogue or stage direction.

Selection of the name in speakers' identification. Most characters have first and last names, even titles, but typing the full name is busywork. To identify the speaker of dialogue, select one name that best represents the character. For example, Oscar Wilde uses Algernon instead of Algernon Moncrieff, and Gwendolen instead of Hon. Gwendolen Fairfax, but he writes Miss Prism instead of Prism, basing decisions on the characters' personalities. Your word processing program may have a handy time-saving device that enters names at the press of a single selected key.

Capital letters. Use all capital letters when the character name appears in stage directions or the heading that indicates who is speaking. Use caps and lowercase when the name appears in dialogue.

Actor Directions

Actor directions are short phrases intended for the person playing the role. Place them one space under the character names, indented eleven spaces from the left margin and enclosed in parentheses. Typical actor directions are (Smiling) (Loudly) (Pointing at him; laughing) and the like.

Variations. You can choose between two rather insignificant variations regarding actor directions. Some playwrights prefer to indent actor directions seven spaces, not eleven. Terminal punctuation, too, is a matter of personal preference: Some writers want to put a period at the end of the actor directions "(Smiling.)" but others don't.

Single and Double Line Spacing

Stage directions are single-spaced, but use a double space to separate paragraphs of directions. Double space after stage directions, before characters' names. Single space between characters' names and actor directions or dialogue. Single space all dialogue. Double space after dialogue before the next stage direction or speaker's name.

Continuation of Speeches

What do you do if a character's dialogue spills over to the next page? You have two choices. First, if the dialogue creates only half a typed line on the next page (called a "widow"), don't spill over. Instead, move the entire speech to the next page. Second, if the dialogue creates more than one typed line on the next page, simply type the character's name and "continued"—SMITH (continued)—at the top of the page.

SAMPLE PAGES FROM A SCRIPT

The following pages show the application of most of the rules regarding script format. You understand, of course, that this published version can't totally replicate a typed manuscript.

<u>TOMORROW IS TOO LATE</u>

A Two-Act Play

by

J. T. Playwright

TOMORROW IS TOO LATE

CAST OF CHARACTERS

MARY LOU QUINCY. 36. Owner of flight school and Fixed Base Operator.

SWASH BUNKER. 32. New York theatre producer.

HECTOR CUNNINGHAM. 33. Mechanic at Quincy Flight School.

THE TIME

The present. Spring.

THE PLACE

Interior of flight school. Alacasta, Mississippi.

Act One. Scene one. Quincy flight school. Morning.

Scene two. Quincy flight school. That afternoon.

Act Two. Scene one. Quincy flight school. The next morning.

Scene two. Quincy flight school. That evening.

TOMORROW IS TOO LATE

ACT ONE

Scene One

SETTING: Painted on a window we see (written backwards) "Quincy Flight School and FBO. M. L. Quincy, Prop." The office is cluttered with airplane pieces and a lot of paper. Walls are decorated with old pictures of airplanes and new photographs of theatre productions and actors. There are several large posters advertising theatrical productions. A computer is on the desk.

AT RISE: Early morning. SOUND: A one-engine plane passes low overhead. Securely tied to a chair is SWASH BUNKER. He is gagged. SWASH wears an expensive World War II leather flying jacket complete with a white scarf around his neck.

MARY LOU QUINCY is moving a floor lamp so it aims at SWASH's eyes. There already is a desk lamp shining in his face. MARY LOU is slim, vigorous, energetic, attractive. She moves and speaks in a staccato rhythm.

HECTOR CUNNINGHAM, dressed in mechanic's overalls, watches MARY LOU.

HECTOR
(Doubtfully.)
Somehow don't seem right, Mary Lou, ropin' down that there tourist.

SWASH
(Through the gag.)
Ummmm mmm MM! (Let me go!)

MARY LOU
What I've got here, Hector, is the Holy Grail.

SWASH
UmmmMMM?! (What?!)

HECTOR
(Studying Swash.)
Don't look all that holy to me.

MARY LOU
All right. Then what I've got here is Jason. The same Jason who got
the Golden Fleece. What I want is a piece of it.

SWASH
Ummm hmmmm. Mmm MMMM! (Oh, God. She's nuts!)

HECTOR
Mary Lou, I swear . . .

MARY LOU
(To Swash.)
I knew you right away, soon as I saw the name on your plane.

SWASH
Ummmmm? (What?)

HECTOR
What name?

HECTOR goes to the window and looks
out.

MARY LOU
"The Swashbuckler."
(To Hector.)
Isn't that what it says on the side of the plane?

HECTOR
(Spelling it out.)
S - W - A -

MARY LOU
(To Swash.)
And you're Mr. Swash Bunker.

                    HECTOR

S - H - B - U - C - K

                    MARY

And now you're mine!

                    SWASH

Ummmmm. (Oh, Lord.)

                    HECTOR

L - E - R. That's Swashbum—Swashluck—

                    MARY LOU

Swash Buckler!

                    HECTOR
            (Trying to understand.)
Didn't you say his name was Swash Bunker?

                    MARY LOU
            (Patting Swash's cheek.)
My own Jason.

                    SWASH

Mmm mmm mm. (Don't touch me.)

                    HECTOR

Jason?

                    MARY LOU

With the Golden Fleece. That's what he's going to give me. Aren't
you?

                    SWASH

Hmmm, hhh MMM! (Lady, you're nuts!)

                    MARY LOU
            (To Hector.)
Turn on that switch.

HECTOR
(Going to the switch.)
I swear I don't understand you sometimes. This poor guy flies in to get gas. Lands out there. Comes in here. You tie him up.

MARY LOU
(Straining to be polite.)
The lights?

HECTOR
Because his name is Swash somethin' or other. Or Jason. Or Fleece.

MARY LOU
(As before.)
Please, Hector?

HECTOR
Like he's the sheep that lays the golden eggs?
(Thinking.)
Sheep? Naw. The chicken that lays . . . No, the . . .

MARY LOU
Hector: LIGHTS ON!

HECTOR
(A bit surprised. Blinking.)
Oh. Right.

HECTOR turns on the switch. The floor lamp goes on. SWASH recoils from the bright light. Both lights are intense, like an interrogation scene.

SWASH
MMMmmm! (Hey!)

MARY LOU
(Thoughtfully.)
I wonder if we need a rubber hose.

                              HECTOR
          (Delighted.)
Like them cop movies? For to hit him with?
          (Almost dancing with delight.)
Violence! Violence!

                              SWASH
Umm Mmm! (No, no!)

                              MARY LOU
          (Pointing at a poster.)
That's your play, isn't it?
          (Reading.)
"Produced by Swash Bunker."
          (Points at another poster.)
And that one. "This play produced by Swash Bunker."
          (Picks up a copy of Variety.)
"Swash Bunker production tops ten mill." Oh, you're a busy pro-
ducer, aren't you? But too busy for really talented writers, huh?

                              HECTOR
          (Awed.)
Ten mill, like . . . like in ten mill?

                              MARY LOU
          (Smiling gently at Swash; the Southern belle.)
And here you are. Dropped in for tea? How nice. How exquisitely,
lovely, perfectly nice. We all, Swash-baby, are goin' to have a party
with you all.

                              SWASH
Ummm? Ummmm. (Party? Ohhhh.)

                              MARY LOU
I do hope ever so much you remember li'l ol' me. Mary Lou Quincy?
Playwright? Author of Tomorrow and Tomorrow? We'll just have to
talk about what you said about my play. Oooo, what horrible, nasty
things. But here you are! Land's sake, Swash-honey, ain't Fate a son
of a bitch?

SWASH

Mmm-mmm. (Oh-oh.)

HECTOR

(Awed.)

This guy's the one you sent your play to? The one who said you oughta burn your typewriter and take up knittin' 'n' cookin' 'n' makin' kids?

MARY LOU

(Grim.)

The very one.

HECTOR

Whooo-EEE! Mister, sayin' somethin' like that to Mary Lou means you gotta be flyin' on half a wing!

MAILING YOUR PLAY

There are two rules regarding giving your play to others. The first is simple: Never let anyone see your play until you are convinced it is as perfect as you can make it. The second rule is even simpler: There are no exceptions to rule number one. A playwright is understandably eager to mail his or her script the moment it is finished, but that eagerness can damage the reputation of a writer who sends a script that can be improved.

Mailing Envelope and Mail-Worn Scripts

Some experts recommend that you protect the appearance of your script by mailing it in a padded envelope. The idea makes sense because you don't want to send out mail-worn scripts that suggest they've been rejected many times, but the padded variety costs more than an ordinary envelope. You'll have to consider the extra expense versus possible damage to your play that may require you to purchase new binders or even have the script copied again. You may find inexpensive mailers listed in advertisements in magazines such as *The Writer* and *Writer's Digest*.

Self-Addressed Stamped Envelope

Always include a self-addressed stamped envelope (SASE) when you send your play. Otherwise it will not be returned to you, and most likely your play simply will be discarded. Worse, it may not even be read: Some producers, directors, publishers, and agents believe that the lack of an enclosed SASE indicates that the writer has an unprofessional attitude.

Self-addressed postcard. You may wish to include a self-addressed, stamped postcard that the recipient can use to acknowledge receipt. Type a simple message such as "We have received your play, TOMORROW IS TOO LATE," and leave room for signature and date. If you're lucky, the recipient may write a brief note indicating when you can expect to receive notice about the fate of your play.

10

Resources for the Playwright

Given the same natural qualifications, he who feels the emotions to be described will be the most convincing; distress and anger, for instance, are portrayed most truthfully by one who is feeling them at the moment. Hence it is that [playwriting] demands a man with a special gift for it, or else one with a touch of madness in him. The former can easily assume the required mood, and the latter may be actually beside himself with emotion.

ARISTOTLE

"A touch of madness" can be valuable while you're writing, as Aristotle suggests in his *Poetics*: the moderately (or perhaps not so moderately) eccentric writer at work, busily talking to invisible characters, gesturing wildly with them as they battle unseen foes, laughing as they relish victories, or crying with their defeats. Relatives and neighbors walk quickly away, looking back over their shoulders at the Strange One. That sort of madness can even be enjoyable.

Unfortunately, however, lunacy also infects the business end of playwriting and many playwrights are perplexed by the complex process—copyrighting your plays, getting an agent, finding details about contests and workshops, locating directors and producers interested in new plays, and estimating potential income from royalties and publication.

An apparent Catch-22 adds to the feeling that theatre is a mad, mad world. Some producers won't consider your play for professional production unless it is submitted by an agent, but many agents won't look at a beginner's work until the playwright has been produced, preferably professionally. More confusing, some play publishers recommend that playwrights explore the rich regional theatre market, but they also say that the best way to get their attention is with a successful production in Manhattan.

Although these circuitous denials appear confusing, they aren't brick walls. In the following pages we look at bright rays of sanity—various resources for the playwright—that can help you find a path through the confusing maze of the business end of playwriting.

Space limitations here prevent complete discussion of all possibilities (entire books are written on these subjects), so in this chapter we look at essential resources, give you basic information, and tell you where you can find additional information. More important, there are constant changes in business procedures, contractual forms, theatrical contests, workshops, organizations, and theatres and producers interested in new plays. Here we show you how and where to find the most recent information.

ORGANIZATIONS FOR PLAYWRIGHTS

Various national and local organizations for playwrights will give you valuable information and advice about contracts, royalties, agents, grants, contests, workshops, seminars, and theatres interested in new plays. Three of the more important organizations are described below.

Dramatists Guild

The Dramatists Guild, created in 1926 by 131 playwrights and originally called the Association of Dramatists, has grown into the primary organization for playwrights, lyricists, and composers, with more than seven thousand members. One of two divisions of the Authors League of America, Inc. (the other is the Authors Guild for book and magazine writers), the Dramatists Guild's numerous professional services deserve the attention of playwrights.

Publications. The Guild publishes the *Dramatists Guild Newsletter* (ten issues annually) and *Dramatists Guild Quarterly*, which lists playwrights' agents in the summer edition. Its annual roundup of producers, agents, contests, and the like is especially valuable; its annual *Directory* informs members about grants, contests, workshops, agents, and production opportunities in New York and regional theatres.

Dramatists Guild contracts. Members receive valuable support and advice regarding theatrical contracts, ranging from Broadway to regional and dinner theatre productions. The Guild's "Approved Production Contract" (which has been in existence since 1985, replacing the "Minimum Basic Production Contract" you may find described in some books) is for first-class productions, with one form for plays and a second for musicals. The Guild also has separate contracts for other productions. These contracts are the theatrical standard for professional production, protecting playwrights in such matters as royalties, the writer's rights in his or her work, and disputes with producers.

Special services. The Guild offers advice about contracts, options, copyrights, taxes, and dealings with producers and agents. It also sponsors seminars and workshops on various business and creative aspects of writing. Members have access to its reference library, health plan, and a telephone hotline for immediate help with contractual problems.

Membership. Two categories of membership are based on the playwright's productions. *Active* Guild members (annual dues currently are $100) have had a minimum of a Broadway, off-Broadway, or regional theatre main stage production. *Associate* members ($65) have written at least one play.

Address and telephone. 234 West 44th Street, Eleventh Floor, New York, New York 10036; (212) 398-9366.

Theatre Communications Group (TCG)

In the 1950s there was a rapid growth of resident nonprofit professional theatres across the nation, stimulated by an increasing desire to decentralize theatre so Manhattan would not be the country's only theatrical headquarters, and made possible by governmental support and the Ford Foundation's multi-million-dollar grants program. The struggles of those regional theatres to survive led to the establishment of the Theatre Communications Group in 1961, also funded by the Ford Foundation. TCG supports regional theatres, provides valuable services to playwrights, and actively encourages production of new plays.

Publications. TCG publishes the annual *Dramatists Sourcebook* (described below under "reference books"); the monthly *American Theatre*, often containing new plays; *Plays in Process/New Plays USA*, volumes containing original plays nominated by theatres affiliated with TCG; *Play Source*, brief descriptions of additional new plays nominated for *Plays in Process* or workshopped by major developmental programs; *ArtSEARCH*, a bulletin of job opportunities in theatre; and *Theatre Profiles*, a guide to more than 200 of TCG's 329 member theatres.

Special programs. TCG sponsors seminars, conferences, and a computerized databank that lists playwrights and other theatre workers. Its "Observership Program" gives playwrights up to $2,000 to live in residence for several weeks of rehearsals while their plays are being prepared for production by one of TCG's constituent theatres, and its "Extended Collaboration Grant" helps playwrights develop works with theatre artists.

Address and telephone. 355 Lexington Avenue, Fourth Floor, New York, New York 10017; (212) 697-5230.

PEN American Center

PEN is a prestigious international literary association of some one hundred centers in major countries that seeks "to promote and maintain friendship and intellectual cooperation among men and women of letters in all countries, in the interests of literature, the exchange of ideas, freedom of expression, and good will." PEN serves as a collective voice for writers, especially those imprisoned or subject to political tyranny. Among notable PEN advocates is playwright Arthur Miller.

Originally for poets, essayists, and novelists (hence the acronym PEN), it now extends membership to playwrights, translators, and editors. Dues currently are $60. PEN has various subcommittees that focus attention on special interests and charities, and it sponsors seminars and workshops.

Publication. PEN American Center publishes *Grants and Awards Available to American Writers*, listing information about financial support such as fellowships, play production, contests, awards, publications, grants, prizes, and writers' colonies. Some international awards are included, and there is a section for Canadian writers.

PEN Prison Writing Program. PEN encourages writers in prisons by sponsoring annual writing awards and publishing winning materials in *The Fortune News*. It also distributes free publications and answers writers' questions and requests for information.
Address and telephone. 568 Broadway, Fourth Floor, New York, New York 10012; (212) 334-1660.

Local Playwrights' Associations

Dramatists' organizations are dedicated to the premise that playwrights can help one another by sharing insight, experience, and play critiques. You'll find strong playwrights' associations affiliated with regional theatres that offer playwrights opportunities for special readings or productions. Other groups may be part of a state or regional writers' club.

You may enjoy the camaraderie of a writer's club with its opportunity to share interests with like-minded people and be part of a mutual support group. Some clubs are primarily social groups, made up of writers who can charitably be called hobbyists. Others show a more serious purpose, sponsoring play readings, contests, seminars with theatre professionals, and script-in-hand or workshop productions. Such organizations can help you make valuable contacts with producers, directors, agents, and publishers.

Locating a writers' organization in your area. Your local theatrical organizations or the reference librarian at your local library may have information about nearby writers' groups. Also consult reference books such as the National Writers Club's *Directory of Local Writers' Organizations* or the *Encyclopedia of Associations*.
Start your own playwrights organization. You can gather other playwrights to form a dramatists group that meets in someone's home perhaps once a month for play readings and critiques. Establish working relationships with local theatres so your group can recruit actors to do script-in-hand readings of new plays and invite directors or other theatre experts to participate in critique sessions. As your plays improve, persuade your local theatres to sponsor workshop readings to invited audiences. From such informal beginnings have sprung a number of significant workshops.

COPYRIGHT

Beginning playwrights often are overly concerned about copyrighting their works to protect against misuse or outright theft, and even experienced playwrights are uncertain about what copyright actually means. In fact, however, as the creator of a play you have certain legal ownership protections without going through the formal copyright registration process, and at any rate a copyright doesn't prevent an unscrupulous director or theatrical company from producing your play without obtaining your permission or paying royalties. Yes, unfortunately, a few dishonest theatres do present plays without paying royalties, but these usually are small-fry producers whose lack of ethics probably extends in other areas that will result in their ultimate collapse.

What Is a Copyright?

Proof of ownership. When you buy a car you register it with your state's department of motor vehicles, receiving a certificate you can use to prove ownership. Equally, a copyright is an international "proof of ownership," showing that you registered your play with the U. S. Copyright Office. Just as your car's title does not mean the state guarantees your car will not be stolen or damaged, so a copyright does not mean the Copyright Office, or any other agency of the United States government, will prosecute anyone suspected of misappropriating your work.

Advantages of Copyrighting Your Play

Registering your play for a copyright gives you grounds for legal actions that you may wish to initiate if your play is produced or published without your permission. Copyright registration carries substantial legal benefits, and in a "worst-case" scenario when you have to resort to the courts, copyright registration is considered *prima facie* evidence. It also gives you legal standing to take actions to stop a misinterpreted production of your play. Samuel Beckett, for example, used copyright registration to stop an all-female production of *Waiting for Godot* (he said that if he had meant it to be done with an all-female cast, he would have written it that way, and he wouldn't permit a wrong-headed director to misinterpret the play). Experts suggest that the relatively small fee for copyrighting a work ($20) is cheap because it gives the playwright the best legal protection available.

Not Eligible for Copyright

Copyright protection does not extend to everything you write. For example, you cannot copyright ideas or titles. More specifically, the United States Copyright Office says the following cannot be copyrighted: "Works that have not been fixed in a tangible form of expression. For example: choreographic works which have not been notated or recorded, or improvisational speeches or performances that have not been written or recorded. Titles, names, short phrases, and slogans; familiar symbols or designs; mere listings of ingredients of contents. Ideas, procedures, methods, systems, processes, concepts, principles, discoveries, or devices, as distinguished from a description, explanation, or illustration. Works consisting entirely of information that is common property and containing no original authorship."

Copyrighting Plays

You can copyright manuscripts of plays and even scenarios, but few playwrights bother to register scenarios because copyright protection is not extended to plays written from them. The Copyright Office defines this category as "published and unpublished works prepared for the purpose of being 'performed' before an audience or indirectly 'by means of any device or process.' Examples of works of the performing arts are: music works, including any accompanying words; dramatic works, including any accompanying music; pantomimes and choreographic works; and motion picture and other audiovisual works."

The Copyright Process

Forms and fees. Copyrighting your play is a relatively simple process. You fill out a simple form, obtainable free on request from the Copyright Office (see address below), and return it with a copy of your play (or two copies if it is published) and the copyright fee (currently $20). The Copyright Office then files your manuscript in its permanent archives and sends you a certificate proving you registered your play. Some playwrights frame the certificates for display in their offices; others store them with important papers for their heirs.

Marking the title page. It's a good idea to indicate to readers that your play is copyrighted by placing on the title page a statement such as: "Copyright (C) 1996 by J. T. Playwright." Better, use the international copyright symbol consisting of a circle around the letter C. You can draw the circle by hand. Some playwrights discourage potential thieves by putting the copyright notice on plays that aren't officially registered with the Copyright Office; the Copyright Office disapproves of this practice, and the lack of official registration eliminates some legal protections.

Duration of copyright. Laws have changed in recent years, giving better protection to authors. As of 1978 a copyright lasts for the author's lifetime plus fifty years.

Publication. You need do nothing if your script is published by one of the play-publishing companies, such as Samuel French and Dramatists Play Service. They will copyright your play. Be sure the copyright is in your name, not the publisher's. Some experts point out, however, that your play may be in the marketplace for some time before it is accepted for publication, which suggests that you're better protected if you copyright your play before placing it in the mail.

Copyright Forms and Informational Materials

The Copyright Office will send you necessary forms and informative brochures such as *Copyright Basics* and *Highlights of the New Copyright Law*. To copyright your play, request *Application Form PA* (Works of Performing Arts). You also can obtain informational kits aimed at special interest areas. Information about drama is contained in Kit 119. Brochures and forms are free.

Address and telephone. Register of Copyrights, Copyright Office, Library of Congress, Washington, D.C. 20559. To request specific forms you can call the Forms Request Hotline, (202) 707-9100 for a recording/message line. The Copyright Office Public Information Office phone number is (202) 707-3000, where information specialists are available from 8:30 A.M. through 5:00 P.M. Monday through Friday.

For Further Information

Author Law and Strategies: A Legal Guide for the Working Writer by Brad Bunnin and Peter Beren (Nolo Press), explains the complexities of copyright law and numerous other business issues facing writers such as contracts, agents, collaborators, publishers, and defamation. Written in easily understood language, the book includes sample agreements, letters, and forms. If you're a professional writer, you probably will want a copy on your bookshelf; alternatively, your local library may have the most recent edition or be able to get a copy for you.

LITERARY AGENTS

Leaders of playwriting workshops and seminars report that the question they encounter most often is not "What should I do to improve my playwriting?" but "How do I get an agent?" The former question has to be answered before the latter: Despite some writers' expectations and hopes, a literary agent cannot jump-start a playwright's career. Agents—more properly, "authors' representatives"—believe you are not ready for representation until you have developed skills, typically through productions in amateur, professional, regional, or off- and off-off Broadway theatres.

What Will an Agent Do?

Your special talent is writing plays; the agent's special talent is knowing the market. Expect a good agent to know precisely which New York or regional theatre producer or director is interested in what particular type of play and to be familiar with foreign markets for your play. The agent submits your playscripts, handles complex business arrangements, represents you, negotiates contracts, ensures your rights are protected so you are treated fairly, makes financial deals in your best interests, and attempts to find solutions to artistic conflicts that may arise. The agent also represents you in movie or television rights and publication. Many good agents will suggest revisions, but they are not playwriting teachers.

The Agent's Economics

The agent receives a certain agreed-upon percentage of the income you receive from scripts he or she handles, usually 10 percent (the norm set forth in the Dramatists Guild's Approved Production Contract) but possibly up to 15 percent, and sometimes up to 20 percent for amateur rights. If your annual playwriting income is, say, $5,000, the agent's percentage would be $500 to $750. That would go toward paying agency salaries, overhead, telephone and fax bills, postage, and other expenses, hardly a profitable proposition for the agent. No wonder they look for playwrights with an established track record. Luckily, most will gamble on new playwrights with long-term promise, preferably with more than one quality script.

When Do You Need an Agent? And When Will an Agent Be Interested in Representing You?

You may want an agent after you have established a production record or have potential for a major production in New York or at a professional regional theatre; or when you have won a major national contest or are recommended by outstanding theatre experts. Agents interested in finding new writing talent often attend playwriting workshop readings or productions.

Agents urge clients to make their own contacts with those working in theatre, primarily directors and producers but certainly actors, designers, and others. Remember that the theatre world is small and overlapping: A director who presents your play at one theatre may move to a different one and recommend you for another production. Most directors and producers feel they have an obligation to replenish the font of theatre literature and are always looking for exciting new plays and new playwrights, and they enjoy discovering a writer and knowing they helped the playwright up the ladder.

Finding an Agent

When you are ready for an agent, seek suggestions from directors, seminar leaders, fellow playwrights, and other theatre personnel with whom you work as your plays are being produced. Participation in workshops often includes introductions to agents. You also can use references that list agents, such as *Literary Market Place, The Dramatists Guild Quarterly, Playwright's Companion*, and *Dramatists Sourcebook*. All are described below. Other helpful books include *Literary Agents: A Writer's Guide* and *Literary Agents of North America*. The *Insider's Guide to Book Editors, Publishers, and Literary Agents* by Jeff Herman describes agents and their interests, even their hobbies, but unfortunately does not include all agents.

Association of Authors' Representatives

In late 1991 the *Society of Authors' Representatives* (SAR) and the *Independent Literary Agents Association* (ILLA) merged to create the *Association of Authors' Representatives* (AAR), a professional organization to establish ethical standards and practices for literary agents. The SAR brochure, *The Literary Agent*, which helped writers locate agents, now is replaced by AAR literature that includes an informational brochure, list of member agents, and a copy of the AAR Canon of Ethics.

Address. Association of Authors' Representatives, Inc., 10 Astor Place, Third Floor, New York, New York 10003; (212) 353-3709.

Contacting an Agent

Agents get testy if you telephone or send unsolicited scripts. A more professional initial approach is a brief (one page maximum) query letter that introduces you, describes your writing and production highlights, indicates your future playwriting plans, and asks if you can send your latest script. Enclose a short (again, one page) description of your play. Be sure to include a self-addressed stamped envelope with your query.

How many agents should you contact at the same time? There's no satisfactory answer. Some agents dislike being one of several you contact, but their all too common delay in replying makes that attitude seem unfair. You might have to wait several months for an answer; if that response is negative, then you must go through the inefficient query-and-wait process all over again. You'll have to decide whether to respect agents' wishes or follow your best interests.

A fair procedure is to query a number of agents, describing your play and its production history. If more than one requests the playscript, give all agents reading the script a reasonable opportunity to respond. If one expresses a strong interest, let other agents know so they can show their interest or return the script.

Advertisements for Critical Services

Beware of advertisements for critical services that imply they will serve as your agent if your script is "good enough." To make your script meet that nebulous standard they'll offer to critique your play, but for a hefty fee. Too often the criticism will not be very helpful and you won't receive the agency representation you seek.

Although a reading fee does not by itself awaken suspicion, some self-proclaimed agents earn more from reading fees than from representing clients, hardly the service you need. Look at such offers with a healthy skepticism and decide if your money will be better spent in a good college playwriting course or at a workshop or seminar.

SOURCES TO HELP YOU FIND PRODUCERS, PUBLISHERS, AGENTS, CONTESTS, AND WORKSHOPS

A number of books can help you find the best market for your play. Most of the following reference books are annuals, containing relatively recent information. Because theatres and publications change submission requirements, and new contests spring to life while older ones disappear, always consult the most recent edition.

Two Valuable Reference Books for Your Personal Library

Two annuals deserve special mention: the *Playwright's Companion* and *Dramatists Sourcebook*. Both are indispensable aids that belong in your library; both are modestly priced paperbacks. Each contains detailed information on literally hundreds of programs, contests, publishers, and theatres or directors interested in new plays. The difficulty of compiling the data staggers the imagination, and all of us in the theatre owe a special debt of gratitude to the editors for what can only be called a labor of love and dedication to helping playwrights. For details regarding all references in this chapter, check these two books for updated information.

The *Playwright's Companion: A Submission Guide to Theatres and Contests in the U.S.A.*, edited by Mollie Ann Meserve, describes theatres, contests, publishers, agents, and special programs for playwrights. Appendices provide helpful cross-listings and a calendar of special events. At one time the *Companion* printed special essays (for example, one edition had a valuable critical review of all playwriting texts), but recent space constraints have eliminated that service. In entries for theatres or contests the *Companion* tells you your chances, indicating the number of plays that are submitted and how many are chosen.

Address. Feedback Theatrebooks, 305 Madison Avenue, Suite 1146, New York, New York 10165.

The annual *Dramatists Sourcebook* is published by Theatre Communications Group, which has its fingers on the pulse of professional theatres across the country. This work contains approximately nine hundred entries that give you details about playwriting contests, agents, publication possibilities, and submission guides to some three hundred theatres. It also describes awards, fellowships, grants, conferences, residencies, and workshops.

Address. Theatre Communications Group, 355 Lexington Avenue, New York, New York 10017.

Basic Reference Book

Writer's Market is a thick volume (over a thousand pages) published by Writers' Digest Books. This annual guide to markets may appear to focus primarily on fiction and nonfiction, but playwrights find valuable entries for scriptwriting, playwriting, theatres looking for new plays, play publishers, contests and awards, and author's agents. Volumes also contain advice about the business of writing, manuscript preparation, mailing, copyright, book contracts, tax regulations, and the like.

Address. Writer's Digest Books, 1507 Dana Avenue, Cincinnati, Ohio 45207.

PERIODICALS

Writers' magazines offer inspiration, helpful writing suggestions, updated market information, and insightful interviews with writers. Some publish concrete "take it to your typewriter" articles that help you improve writing characterization, structure, and dialogue. Others focus on new developments and theatrical concepts. You'll find some of the following periodicals in your local library, and you'll want to consider subscribing to one or more.

American Theatre

Theatre articles, reviews, and interviews are found in Theatre Communications Group's monthly magazine focused on professional not-for-profit theatres in the United States. A special section announces results of playwriting competitions and describes forthcoming grants, contests, and other opportunities for playwrights. It publishes half a dozen new plays annually.

Address. 355 Lexington Avenue, New York, New York 10017.

The Writer

A monthly magazine for writers, *The Writer* publishes instructional articles, interviews, and inspirational materials that can help overcome motivational obstacles that plague creative workers. Although most pieces are aimed at authors of fiction and nonfiction, the contents can help you develop characters and shape your play. Look here, too, for latest information about play contests.

Address. 120 Boylston Street, Boston, Massachusetts 02116.

Writer's Digest

Writer's Digest, a monthly, aims at poets, novelists, nonfiction authors, and playwrights. Interviews with writers discuss techniques and tips. Regular columns focus on specific aspects of writing such as poetry, screenwriting, and so forth, which can help you recharge your creative batteries and inspire you to return to your project with renewed enthusiasm. Note in particular its advertisements for *Writer's Digest Books*, a large collection for writers.

Address. 9933 Alliance Road, Cincinnati, Ohio 45242.

Dramatics

Published monthly September through May, *Dramatics* magazine features new plays and articles on various aspects of theatre including playwriting. Although it is intended for secondary schools, many pieces are written by theatre professionals and college/university professors. Interviews often feature playwrights.

Address. 3368 Central Parkway, Cincinnati, Ohio 45225.

Theater

Published three times annually by the Yale School of Drama and the Yale Repertory Theater, *Theater* contains plays with associated production photographs, essays, and interviews with the playwrights.

Address. 222 York Street, New Haven, Connecticut 06520.

The Drama Review (formerly Tulane Drama Review)

TDR, a quarterly, focuses on avant-garde movements, emphasizing theatrical work in a broad-based intercultural and interdisciplinary context including political and anthropological frameworks. **Address.** MIT Press Journals, 55 Hayward Street, Cambridge, Massachusetts 02142.

CONTESTS, WORKSHOPS, SEMINARS, AND CONFERENCES

Several hundred organizations, dedicated to helping playwrights develop their plays, sponsor contests, workshops, seminars, and conferences. These give you valuable opportunities to meet theatre directors, producers, agents, and other playwrights and to establish contacts that can help you in the future.

Submission requirements. Well before announced deadlines, write for application forms, rules, eligibility requirements, and other details. Enclose a self-addressed stamped envelope. Read specifications carefully; there's no point in sending a play that sponsors will not consider.

For further information regarding contests, workshops, and the like, look in the *Playwright's Companion* and *Dramatists Sourcebook*. Also read current magazines such as *American Theatre, The Writer,* and *Writer's Digest.*

Contests and Prizes

A number of playwriting contests are open each year—TCG lists 140 with cash awards of over $200, and other contests are available with lesser prizes or awards other than cash—giving you opportunities for prizes, production, or publication, and frequently a combination of cash awards and production. Winners of contests involving production usually receive stipends for travel, room, and board so they can attend rehearsals of their plays. Cash awards range from several hundred dollars to $5,000 or $6,000.

Suggestions. Speaking as a judge of contests that have drawn several hundred plays, I urge you to remember that judges are forced to look for reasons to eliminate the majority of the entries. Therefore you should carefully type your manuscript in standard playwriting format. Never send a script with misspellings, typos, or grammatical errors (unless they depict the character). Neatness is important. It's good strategy to enter your play well before the deadline to give readers a chance to study it before they are deluged with entries. Consider including a concise (one or two paragraphs) outline of the play but avoid hyper-cute descriptions of your play: "A hilarious modern comedy-tragedy in a new-old Greek-French classic style that the playwright's friends loved and you will, too" is guaranteed to put your play, unread, at the bottom of the pile. Enclose a large self-addressed stamped envelope so your play will be returned.

Read rules carefully. Some contests are open to any entry. Others specify the type of play they'll accept, such as one-acts, full-lengths, musicals, translations, or plays for young audiences. Contests occasionally search for plays dealing with certain themes, defined in annual announcements (yet another reason to obtain contest rules well in advance).

Advantages in entering contests. Cash awards are attractive, but there are other reasons to enter contests. Prestigious contests draw attention to you and your work, opening possibilities of future productions, and there's a chance a contest judge may find your play attractive for his or her theatrical organization.

If you don't win. Don't let a rejection disappoint you. Contests may have three or five judges, and experience indicates that "winners" seldom are any single judge's first choice but instead are selected by a mathematical averaging system, which means first prize might go to a play that no judge ranked very highly. Each judge may have selected a different "first place" script, yet under the averaging system those plays might not receive even honorable mention; and you may not even know that your play was high on one judge's list. If you have faith in your play, enter it in another contest.

Workshops and Conferences

Some fifty "new play" workshops and conferences in various parts of the country are dedicated to developing playwrights and playscripts, often providing stipends for room, board, and travel to the site. These are valuable experiences, well worth your consideration.

While each workshop has different goals and operations, most require that you have at least one completed script to be studied and revised while you're in residence for several weeks, often during the summer, working closely with playwrights, directors, actors, or critics. Most put your play "on its feet" in a staged reading. Discussions identify your play's strengths and weaknesses, and you receive suggestions for revisions. You also will make valuable contacts with potential producers, directors, and agents.

Application. Details are listed in the *Playwright's Companion, Dramatists Sourcebook,* and periodicals such as *The Writer* and *Writer's Digest.* Because programs may change policies or operations, you should write for information, sending your request well before the program's announced deadlines (remember to enclose a SASE).

PRODUCTIONS

Playwrights may dream of a star-studded Broadway performance that brings fame and fortune, but an examination of Broadway's offerings leads one to the conclusion that today's producers seldom favor new plays and are even less interested in new playwrights. Moreover, critics complain that Broadway producers prefer British imports over American works. It's a distinctly shabby situation for American theatre.

Alternatives to Broadway

If Broadway closes itself off to new plays, however, an active theatrical decentralization process opens numerous other production possibilities that deserve your attention. Many off- and off-off Broadway organizations, as well as regional theatres across the country, are dedicated to new playwrights and have given now well-known playwrights their start. You also can receive excellent productions in community and college theatres. These experiences can build your morale, give you motivation to continue writing, and help you improve your plays.

Off- and Off-Off Broadway

Off-Broadway began, if a date can be attached to a movement that did not instantly spring full-grown into existence, in 1952 with José Quintero's production of Tennessee Williams's poetic drama of loneliness, *Summer and Smoke,* presented at the Circle in the Square in Greenwich Village. At least that was the first non-Broadway show to receive a major review in the *New York Times,* legitimizing a movement that offered a lively alternative to the increasingly stale Broadway fare.

Despite popular opinion, off-Broadway is not a geographic region in Manhattan but is more an economic arrangement between producers and theatrical unions, based on the number of seats available for sale. Unions such as Actors Equity, which sets salaries for professional actors, agreed to establish a lower pay scale for auditoriums with a seating capacity of 499 or fewer (off-Broadway) than the standard higher scale for houses with 500 or more (Broadway). Typical off-Broadway theatres seat fewer than 200 people. The agreement frees professional actors to perform in low-budget off-Broadway shows. In Manhattan there are more of the small-size auditoriums than the large, thus more off-Broadway houses and, by extension, more theatrical productions that use the abundant talent pool of actors, directors, designers, and technicians. And—important for you—more opportunities to have your play produced in New York.

Through the 1950s and into the 1960s, off-Broadway's advantage was its freedom from various theatrical unions' economic pressures for high salaries, coupled with visionary writers, directors, actors, and producers who wanted to create an alternative to Broadway's focus on smooth commercial fare that neglected controversial or new ideas. Off-Broadway started on the proverbial shoestring, and many theatres mounted productions for less than $500, which meant they could be economically sound even with relatively small audiences. But theatre followed its normal hunger to grow, and by the end of the 1960s production costs soared to over $15,000, requiring larger audiences, which in turn shifted focus to commercially-based plays. Off-Broadway began to look like Broadway's clone. Production costs now can range from $250,000 to $500,000, turning what was an iconoclastic free-spirited off-Broadway movement into a commercial organization like Broadway.

Off-Off Broadway. Logically, then, off-off Broadway was born. Prompted by the same vision that started off-Broadway, and with major concessions from unions such as Actors Equity, the movement again is a factor of the maximum number of auditorium seats—in this case, no more than 99 seats. Off-off Broadway theatre means churches, lofts, basements, and warehouses. Small theatres sprang up, as many as 150 at one time. Chief among them was La Mama, founded in 1961 by Ellen Stewart, which presented a large number of plays and gave a hearing to many new playwrights such as Sam Shepard. Representative contemporary playwrights who received their start in off-off Broadway include Spalding Gray, author of the monodrama *Swimming to Cambodia*, and Lanford Wilson, known for one-acts such as *Ludlow Fair* and full-lengths such as *Talley's Folly*. Although they are low-budget and nonprofit organizations, off-off Broadway theatres provide excellent opportunities for playwrights.

You'll find that off-off Broadway is open to original plays, ranging from traditional realism to experimental or avant-garde, and that a strong core of producers, directors, and actors are eager to stage works by new playwrights. Some organizations, however, claim to be interested in original plays but in fact are interested only in plays by their own staff members, and you discover current attitudes only through tiresome applications and queries.

Although making contacts is easier if you live in the area, at conferences and seminars you'll meet actors and directors who are eager to work off-off Broadway and might be interested in your scripts. Also refer to your standard reference books—*Dramatists Sourcebook* and the *Playwright's Companion*—for names and addresses.

Regional Theatres

As the decentralization process gave birth to off-Broadway, equally strong motivations started the regional theatre movement. Today there are more than three hundred not-for-profit professional regional theatres across the nation, bringing new excitement to our art.

Regional theatres are known for their professionalism and excellence, represented by such organizations as Arena Stage (Washington), Goodman Theatre (Chicago), and the Mark Taper Forum (Los Angeles). Some, like the Yale Repertory Theatre and the Actors Theatre of Louisville, present annual new play festivals. Regional theatres also present workshop productions and readings of new plays in small studio theatres. Some regional theatres premiere new plays that ultimately become New York successes.

If you believe you have a stageworthy script, make personal contacts with the regional theatre nearest you. You may have to be persistent to catch the attention of directors and actors, but the end result can be an excellent production of your play. Also refer to the basic reference books for information on other regional theatres.

A Do-It-Yourself Showcase Production

A showcase production is aptly named: It exhibits talent. Playwrights, actors, and directors frequently sponsor showcase productions in New York's off-off Broadway theatres, using small auditoriums, keeping expenses to a minimum, perhaps financing the performances themselves or finding sponsors. The stage experience helps theatre artists develop their skills. Showcases also give them valuable exposure, and they make a special point of inviting critics, producers, directors, and agents.

Showcase productions aren't limited to New York residents. Even if you don't live in New York, you can put together an off-off Broadway showcase production of your play, using actors and directors you've met through various seminars, conventions, and productions. If that isn't possible, by all means consider a showcase production in your local facilities such as a public library, community theatre, high school auditorium, coffeehouse, or the like, perhaps in association with your local dramatists club or community or university theatre. Invite local theatre experts to attend and discuss the production. The showcase puts your play on its feet in the crucible of audience response, thereby helping you improve your writing skills, and it can lead to subsequent productions.

INCOME

Your playwriting income is based on royalties from professional or amateur performances and publication. Income varies so widely that cynical playwrights cite playwright Robert Anderson's wry observation: "The theatre is the only business where you can make a killing but not a living." Most playwrights support their writing habit with other jobs. What income can you expect? We look at some possibilities below.

Royalties for Broadway and Regional Theatre Production

The Dramatists Guild works with the League of American Theaters and Producers to establish an "Approved Production Contract" for plays and musicals. For a first-class production, staged on Broadway or in large theatres, the APC contract specifies that playwrights will receive a minimum of five percent royalties on prerecoupment of expenses—"recoupment" is the point when one hundred percent of production expenses have been earned back out of weekly operating profit—and ten percent for postrecoupment. Similar percentages apply to out-of-town tryouts.

For successful Broadway productions this can translate into a playwright's weekly income of approximately $4,000 to $26,000, depending of course on variables such as the play's popularity, the amount of initial capitalization, weekly operating expenses, and gross weekly box office receipts. Such categories fluctuate a great deal, not only from play to play but from week to week as well.

Nonprofit regional theatres generally pay playwrights six percent to ten percent of ticket sales, although some may lower the rate to five percent for untested new playwrights. You may receive $6,000 to $10,000 for a relatively successful play at a regional theatre, and that exposure can open possibilities for added productions elsewhere.

Royalties for Amateur Production

Reputable educational and community theatres are sensitive to the new playwright's economic problems and will attempt to pay as much as possible for premieres. That can translate into several thousand dollars. Such theatres try to provide funds for you to be present during the production process.

Some amateur theatres may offer you an amount equal to what they'd pay for a "professional" play from a major play publisher or leasing agent. For a full-length play, that is usually $50 for the first performance and $35 for each subsequent performance. One-act plays may receive $25/$15.

Beware of theatres that suggest they not pay you at all, implying that they are doing you a favor by producing your script or claiming they have inadequate funds. *Nonsense.* That attitude quite likely reflects equally undesirable attitudes about other aspects of producing your play, and it's difficult to imagine a reason for a playwright to accept such conditions unless the company pays no one else, has the theatre rent-free, and has cut all production expenses (including cast parties!) to bare minimums.

Playwright-in-Residence: Commissioned Works

A few theatres dedicated to new works offer residencies, commissioning a playwright to write a new play or agreeing to produce the author's existing play. In either case, the theatre wants you present from preplanning through auditions and rehearsals to production. Such theatres usually pay transportation as well as room and board for perhaps five to eight weeks. You work with director, cast, and designers; more important for your growth as a playwright, you use rehearsals to revise your script as necessary. In some cases you may be required to lead playwriting seminars or workshops. The amount varies with the theatre's financial resources but may be as much as $6,000.

PUBLICATION

Publication and production make a circle; one often leads to the other. Your play may be published by a magazine, such as *Dramatics*, or a play publisher, such as Samuel French or Dramatists Play Service. You'll be paid in either case, although the amount varies a great deal; more important, publication means your play will be visible to a number of readers and potential producers. You'll find some one hundred possible publishers listed in *Dramatists Sourcebook*, *Playwright's Companion*, and *Writer's Market*.

Magazine Publication

Magazines seek plays for their readers, not necessarily producers. They typically buy rights for only one issue; they are not involved with any aspect of performance. All rights revert to you after publication, allowing you to seek production or further publication with a play publisher. The magazine does not take a percentage of your income from such sources.

Your potential income. Maximum payment is several hundred dollars. You'll also receive free copies of the issue in which your play appears.

Selecting magazines to which you can submit your play. First learn each magazine's policies before sending your script. Start by studying a number of magazines, paying careful attention to the plays they've published. Then examine market guides that describe magazines' requirements, using the basic reference books listed above. Select the magazine that appears most likely to be interested in your play's length, content, and style.

Play Publishers

Play publishers print your play in an acting edition for directors and actors, and they handle production rights by leasing your play to theatres and collecting royalties for performances. They are your best bet for numerous productions. Most publishers are primarily interested in plays that have had at least one successful production.

Your potential income. You receive royalties from book sales and productions. A typical contract offers you ten percent royalties from book sales, eighty percent of performance royalties paid by amateur theatres, and ninety percent of the performance rights paid by stock companies. Publishers usually pay you an advance against predicted income and send you ten free copies of your play (thereafter you'll have to purchase copies of your play from them, usually at a forty percent discount).

A few play publishers offer you a negotiable one-time payment, perhaps $200 or $300, to purchase all rights to your play; you then do not receive future income from book or production royalties or sale of subsidiary rights. Experts suggest that you should not sell your play outright, so think very carefully before signing away your play.

Selecting play publishers to which you can submit your play. Start by examining each publisher's catalog. Most play publishers will send you a free catalog; basic reference books list addresses. Although catalogs are designed for producers and directors, playwrights find them a helpful indicator of each publisher's basic specialization, such as Broadway successes, children's plays, religious drama, and the like. Then study the market guides that describe publishers' policies. Send your script to publishers that seem most apt to be interested in your play's length, content, and style.

CONCLUSION

One conclusion can be stated simply: Be persistent. You learn to improve your writing from seeing your plays in rehearsals and productions, which means you must think of yourself as your own sales expert, taking all possible steps to get your plays staged. Think of marketing as a do-it-yourself project—after all, a play sitting in your file cabinet can't get a production. Take advantage of the many options we've described. Be patient. While you're developing your skills, don't expect immediate professional production but instead find other avenues, including self-production in local showcases.

A second conclusion also is simple: Make contacts. Develop working relationships with playwrights, producers, directors, and actors. That isn't as distasteful as it may sound to those who believe their plays should speak for themselves. The theatrical world is a small, close-knit community, more supportive of its members than outsiders recognize, and theatre people you meet in one situation can recommend your plays in other environments. Be active in your local theatres. Attend workshops, seminars, and conferences. You'll meet interesting people and find a great deal of support.

Finally, don't be imprisoned by the "Broadway mentality." Of course playwrights dream of a Broadway production with a star-studded, super-glitzy opening and the postshow party at a famed watering hole while waiting for the reviews. Broadway's legends and excitement are powerful attractions. We hope you make it there. But it is a mistake to expect your first play—or even your first half-dozen plays—to become part of the Broadway legend. First you must pay your dues, learning your art and craft through writing a number of plays, in effect serving an apprenticeship in an educational process no less important than that demanded of doctors and lawyers. Don't think that a Broadway production is the only measure of your success as a playwright. Instead think of *production* as your goal—production in your own town, in educational and community theatres, children's groups, religious organizations, and in regional theatres.

We started this chapter with a reference to "a touch of madness." It is appropriate to conclude the chapter, and this book, with a different tone:

> *Children, you must remember something. A man without ambition is dead. A man with ambition but no love is dead. A man with ambition and love for his blessings here on earth is ever so alive. Having been alive, it won't be hard in the end to lie down and rest.*
>
> —Pearl Bailey

Good luck and good writing!

Writers at Work
(Part Two)

STAN: We could be the greatest, Gene. The greatest comedy writers in
America. . . . I just have to learn to deal with the pressure.
EUGENE: So do I. It's not easy for me either.
STAN: I'm feeling better. I'm glad we had this talk. It reassures me
that you want to stick with me. I'm feeling more relaxed now.
EUGENE: So am I.
STAN: . . . Now if we can just get an idea.

NEIL SIMON
Broadway Bound

Index

Acting techniques to help playwrights, 67–70

Action, 23, 57; and characterization, 65–66; and dialogue, 126–127; and point of attack, 105; structure of, 60–61, 105; and theme, 19–20; unity of, 30–33

Actor directions, 149–150, 176

Actors Theatre of Louisville, 41, 204

Acts: ending with suspense, 115; number of, 44–45

After the Fall (Miller), 73

Agents, 194–197

Agnes of God (Pielmeier), 137, 138–139

Albee, Edward, 27, 38, 40, 41, 43, 69, 115, 126, 144, 148

Allen, Jay Presson, 38

All My Sons (Miller), 153

Amadeus (Shaffer), 52

American Theatre (magazine), 189

Anderson, Maxwell, 142

Anderson, Robert, 46, 101–106

Antagonist, 22–23, 80–81, 163–164

Approved Production Contract, 188

Aristotle, 30–31, 118–119, 123, 186

Association of Authors' Representatives (AAR), 196

Audience, 45–46; and imagination, 29–30, 128; response of, 87, 168–169

Author Law and Strategies (Bunnin and Beren), 193

Authors League of America, 187

Author's representatives, 194–197

Autobiographical writing, 39, 72–74

Awards for writers, 189

Bailey, Pearl, 210

Barrie, James M., 28

Beckett, Samuel, 30, 38, 40, 69, 78, 105, 118, 150, 191

Beginning of a play, 26, 61, 95–96, 96–104; revising, 167

Beliefs, writing from, 3–6, 53; dialogue and, 127

Beren, Peter, 193

Biloxi Blues (Simon), 73

Bogosian, Eric, 39

Bradford, Benjamin, 67

Brecht, Bertolt, 28, 29

Bridge of San Luis Rey, The (Wilder), 11

Brighton Beach Memoirs (Simon), 73, 150

Broadway, xvii–xviii, 46, 202, 209; royalties paid, 205–206

Broadway Bound (Simon), 32, 73

Brown, Arvin, 10

Bully! (Alden), 39

Bunnin, Brad, 193

Burn This (Wilson), 86, 87

Camelot (Lerner and Loewe), 108

Canadian Gothic (Glass), 33, 43
Candida (Shaw), 136, 149–150
Capote, Truman, 36
Caretaker, The (Pinter), 68
Castelvetro, Ludovico, 31
Catharsis, 95, 118–119
Cave Dwellers, The (Saroyan), 69
Character: contribution to plot,
    65; as idea for play, 50, 52; as
    mask of dramatic action, 82;
    motivating entrances of, 114–
    115; number of, 39, 42, 44–
    45, 89–91; primacy of, 64–65;
    sources for, 71–75
Characterization writing tech-
    niques: 64–93; action, 66, 70;
    age, 66–67; amplifying, 56–
    57; appearance, 68; biog-
    raphy, 70–71; clues to, 66–
    67; conflict, 24; descriptions
    by others, 71; dialogue, 128–
    130; emotions, 86–87; envi-
    ronment, 68–69; names, 68;
    physical mannerisms, 68; re-
    vising, 162, 163–164; self-
    definition, 71; vocal manner-
    isms, 68
Characters, types of: antago-
    nist, 80–81, 163–164; central,
    60; confidant(e), 85; contrast-
    ing, 87; necessary for play,
    75–85, 89–91; opposing, 60;
    pivotal, 85; protagonist, 76–
    80, 162–163; secondary, 82–
    85; unconventional, 64, 88, 89
Chekhov, Anton, 68, 71, 100–
    101
Cherry Orchard, The (Chekhov),
    68
Chorus Line, A (Kirkwood), 11
Climax, 95, 104, 107, 116; and
    major dramatic question, 116
Closet drama, 7–8
Coburn, D. L., 67–68
Come Blow Your Horn (Simon),
    153
Complications, 95, 104, 107–
    115; entrances as, 110–112;

exits as, 112–114; number of,
    109–110
Conduct of Life, The (Fornes), 73
Confessions of a Nightingale
    (Chandler and Stricklyn), 39
Confidant(e), 85
Conflict, 22–25, 42, 60, 65, 80,
    100, 102, 103, 104; and char-
    acterization, 24; with charac-
    ters, 65; and dialogue, 123–
    127; in full-length plays, 45;
    and meaning of play, 23; in
    monodramas, 40; secondary,
    45; and structure of play, 24
Contests for playwrights, 200–
    201
Contractions in dialogue, 137–
    138
Contrast in dialogue, 139, 143
Copyright, 191–194
Copyright Basics (Library of
    Congress), 193
Coward, Noël, 1
Crimes of the Heart (Henley), 44,
    89
Critical services, paying for,
    196–197
Cronyn, Hume, 136
Crucible, The (Miller), 53, 73,
    80–81, 85, 89
Cyrano de Bergerac (Rostand),
    71, 84, 85, 123

Dance and the Railroad, The
    (Hwang) 43, 73
Davis, Bill C., 161
Death of a Salesman (Miller),
    31–33, 78, 85, 101, 116, 127,
    141–142
Denouement, 95, 118
Desperate Hours, The (Hayes), 51
Deux ex machina, 117–118
Dialogue: as action, 123, 126–
    127; characterization and,
    128–130; conflict in, 124,
    126–127; ear for, 122, 130–
    132; literary, 125; offstage,

150; theatrical, compared with other forms, 123–125

Dialogue writing techniques, 122–152; clichés, 146–147; to communicate to audience, 19–20; ellipsis, 136–137; incomplete sentences, 137–138; junk words, 146; length of sentences and speeches, 147–148; in monologue, 144–145; present and past tense, 146; pronouns, 135; revising, 164–165; rule of three, 134; specifics, 135; structural emphasis in sentences, 139–142; vocabularies, 123–124; vocal mannerisms of characters, 68

Directions, playwright's to actor, 149–50, 176

Discoveries, 114–115. *See also* Complications

Do-it-yourself production, 205, 209

Doll's House, A (Ibsen), 23, 57–58, 78

Drama Review, The (journal), 199–200

Dramatics (magazine), 199

Dramatists Guild, 187–188

Dramatists Guild Newsletter and *Quarterly*, 187

Dramatists Play Service, 207

Dramatists Sourcebook (Theatre Communications Group), 189, 197–198, 202, 207

Drinking in America (Bogosian), 39

Dumbwaiter, The (Pinter), 30, 126–127

Durang, Christopher, 53, 157

Edgar, David, 44

Elephant Man, The (Pomerance), 68

Eliot, T. S., xviii, 142

Ellipses in dialogue, 136–137

Emotions, 29, 59, 77–78; and dialogue, 127

Ending of play, 26, 59, 61–62, 95–96; revising, 168; surprise-type, 119

Entrances, 100, 110–112; sustaining, 111–112

Environment, influence on characters, 68–70

Equilibrium, 95, 101, 104

Euripides, 23, 89, 98, 99, 105

Exits, 112–114

Exposition, 95, 98–99, 101, 102, 103

Faulkner, William, 63

Fiddler on the Roof (Stein, Harnick, and Bock), 143

Fierstein, Harvey, 53

Fifth of July (Wilson), 86

Fool for Love (Shepard), 32, 78, 89, 105, 128

Foreshadowing, 95, 100, 101, 110

Fornes, Maria Irene, 73

Fortune News, The (PEN publication), 190

Fountainhead, The (Rand), 5

Fratti, Mario, 72

French Fries (Martin), 40

Fry, Christopher, 142

Fuller, Charles, 44, 52

Full-length play, 43–45, 46, 95–96, 109

Funny Thing Happened on the Way to the Forum, A (Sondheim, Shevelove, and Gelbart), 109

Future tense, 20, 61, 146

García Lorca, Federico, 142

Germinal ideas for a play, 50, 52; developing, 53–59

Gertrude Stein Gertrude Stein Gertrude Stein (Martin), 39

Ghosts (Ibsen), 32, 99

Gin Game, The (Coburn), 67–68

Glass, Joanna, 33, 41, 43

Glass Menagerie, The (Williams), 84, 87, 99, 105, 112–114, 138, 140–141, 142, 144, 154

Goldberg, Whoopi, 39
Goodman Theatre, 204
Good Times/Bad Times (Kirk-wood), 11
Grants and awards for writers, 189
Gray, Spalding, 39, 204
Great Nebula in Orion, The (Wilson), 58–59
Gurney, A. R., Jr., 157

Hairy Ape, The (O'Neill), 69, 129
Hamlet (Shakespeare), 24, 97, 101, 105, 106, 116, 118, 127
Hansberry, Lorraine, 44
Harvey (Chase), 28, 30
Hayes, Joseph, 51
Hedda Gabler (Ibsen), 85
Hellman, Lillian, 39, 75, 157, 169
Hemingway, Ernest, 124, 154
Henley, Beth, 44, 89, 127, 130
Herman, Jeff, 195
Highlights of the New Copyright Law (Library of Congress), 193
Holbrook, Hal, 39
Hopscotch (Horovitz), 42, 43
Horovitz, Israel, 42
Hot L Baltimore, The (Wilson), 69, 86, 89
Howe, Tina, 71, 72, 155
Hunt, Linda, 136
Hwang, David Henry, 43, 73

Ibsen, Henrik, 23, 32, 57–58, 78, 85, 99
Iceman Cometh, The (O'Neill), 69
Ideas for plays, 49–63; ampli-flying, 55–59; sources for, 50–59, 74–75; structuring, 60–61; theatrical potential of, 59–62
Imagery, 142–144
Imagination, audience, 29–30, 128
Importance of Being Earnest, The (Wilde), 69, 115–116, 128
Improvisations, 158–159

Incidents: in full-length plays, 45; in one-act plays, 42
Inciting incident, 97–98, 101–103, 107
Income, playwright's, 205
Incomplete sentences in dia-logue, 136–138
Independent Literary Agents Association, 196
I Never Sang for My Father (Anderson), 46
Inge, William, 13
In medias res, 47
Insider's Guide to Book Editors, Publishers, and Literary Agents (Herman), 195
Interruptions in dialogue, 138
Introduction to Theatre, An (Whiting), 2
Investigation, The (Weiss), 23
Ionesco, Eugène, 18, 41, 44

Journal, playwright's, 15–16. *See also* Writer's notebook
Junk words in dialogue, 146

King Lear (Shakespeare), 28, 81, 127
Kirkwood, James, 11
Knott, Frederick, 51
Krapp's Last Tape (Beckett), 40

Lardner, Ring, 16
Length of plays, 36–46, 95–96
Library of Congress, 193
Life and Adventures of Nicholas Nickleby, The (Edgar), 44
Lillian (Luce), 39
Literary agents, 194–197
Literary writing, compared with theatrical writing, 124, 125
Little Foxes, The (Hellman), 157
Long Day's Journey into Night (O'Neill), 73
Long sentences in dialogue, 147–148

Lovely Light, A (Stickney), 39
Lowell, James Russell, 63
Ludlow Fair (Wilson), 71, 145, 204

Macbeth (Shakespeare), 42, 58, 78, 89, 100, 105, 116, 129, 141
McLure, James, 43
Madness of Lady Bright, The (Wilson), 145
Magazine publication for playwrights, 207–208
"Magic if," the, 58–59
Mailing plays, 185
Major dramatic question, 101, 104, 106–107, 116
Mamet, David, 41
Mansfield, Katherine, xviii
Marat/Sade (Weiss), 84
Markets for plays, 46; Broadway, 46, 202; contests, 200–201; off-Broadway, 46, 202–203; off-off Broadway, 46, 202–204; publishers, 207–208; regional theatre, 204–205; royalties, 205–206. *See also* Resources for playwrights
Mark Twain Tonight! (Holbrook), 39
Martin, Jane, 38, 40, 135
Mason, Marshall W., 10
Mass Appeal (Davis), 161
Maugham, W. Somerset, 121
Medea (Euripides), 23, 89, 98, 99, 105
Meserve, Mollie Ann, 197
Middle (of play), 26, 61, 95–96, 104–117; revising, 167–168
Miller, Arthur, 14, 31–32, 35, 52, 53, 73, 78, 80–81, 85, 89, 101, 116, 127, 141, 142, 153, 189
Minimum Basic Production Contract, 188
Minnesota Moon (Olive), 42, 43
Miser, The (Molière), 23
Molière, 23

Monodrama, 32, 38–41, 45, 109, 123, 135; characteristics of, 39–40; strengths and weaknesses of, 41
Monologue, 123, 144–145
Mood setting, 101, 105
Mourning Becomes Electra (O'Neill), 44, 153
My Fair Lady (Lerner and Loewe), 143
My Heart's in the Highlands (Saroyan), 127

Nabokov, Vladimir, 155
Narrator, use of for exposition, 99
News stories, as sources for characters, 74–75
No Exit (Sartre), 42, 53, 88, 110–111, 144
Noises Off (Frayn), 109
Norman, Marsha, 93
Novel writing, compared to theatrical writing, 11–12, 18–22, 124
Number of characters in a play, 39, 42, 44–45, 89–91

Obstacles, *see* Complications
Octavia (Seneca), 8
Odd Couple, The (Simon), 52, 74
Oedipus Rex (Sophocles), 69
Off-Broadway, 46, 202–203
Off-off Broadway, 46, 202–204
Olive, John, 42
Olivier, Laurence, 67
One-act play, 37–38, 41–43, 46, 109; length, 41–42; parts of, 96; strengths and weaknesses of, 43; unified into full-length, 46, 53
O'Neill, Eugene, 41, 44, 69, 73, 129, 153
Our Town (Wilder), 11, 99, 127

Painting Churches (Howe), 72, 155
Pasternak, Boris, 59

Past tense, 20, 39–40; in dialogue, 146
PEN American Center, 189–190
Period of Adjustment (Williams), 146
Peter Pan (Barrie), 28
Pielmeier, John, 137, 138–139
Pinter, Harold, 30, 68, 98, 126
Pivotal character, 85
Place, unity of, 30–33
Plant (item in play), 100
Plato, 8, 29
Plays in Process/New Plays USA (Theatre Communications Group), 189
Play Source (Theatre Communications Group), 189
Playwright: and dialogue, 122, 130–132; goal of, 162; heritage of, 1–3; journal, 15, 54–55; and observation, 72; purpose of, 33–34; work habits of, 10–13
Playwrights' associations, 187–190, 196
Playwright's Companion, The (Meserve), 197–198, 202, 207
Playwriting (Catron), 4–5
Plaza Suite (Simon), 46
Plot: and characterization, 65; divisions of, 95–96; primacy of, 64–65; three parts of, 95
Plot complications, *see* Complications
Plot writing techniques, 94–121; beginning, 101–104; catharsis, 118–119; continuum in time, 97; denouement, 118; *deus ex machina*, 117–118; end, 95; ending acts with suspense, 115; entrances, 111–112; equilibrium, 101; exits, 112–114; exposition, 98–99; foreshadowing, 100; inciting incident, 97–98; introductory material, 95, 96–104; middle, 95, 104–117; plant, 100; revising, 162, 165–168; situation, 51–52, 56–57
Poetics (Aristotle), 30–31, 118–119, 186
Poetry, 124, 142–144
Point of attack, 79, 95, 101, 103, 104–106, 107; play's first complication, 108
Pomerance, Bernard, 68
Porter, Katherine Anne, 59
Poster of the Cosmos, A (Wilson), 40–41
Present tense, 20, 61, 66, 107; in dialogue, 146
Price, The (Miller), 52
Prison Writing Program, 190
Production contracts, 188
Protagonist, 22–25, 76–80, 163; goal of, 22, 78–79, 95, 101, 102, 103, 104, 106, 107; plan, 79–80
P.S. Your Cat Is Dead! (Kirkwood), 11
Publications for playwrights, 187, 189, 197–200, 207–208
Publishers, play, 207–208
Pvt. Wars (McLure), 43

Raisin in the Sun, A (Hansberry), 44
Rand, Ayn, 5
Regional theatre, 46, 157, 204–205
Resources for playwrights, 186–210
Revisions, 22, 152, 153–169; using improvisations, 158; working with others, 156–161
Rhinoceros (Ionesco), 44
Richards, Lloyd, 10
Riders to the Sea (Synge), 41
Romeo and Juliet (Shakespeare), 22, 52, 107, 108
Rostand, Edmond, 71, 84, 85, 123
Royalties, 205–208
Rule of three in dialogue, 134
R.U.R. (Čapek), 28

Samuel French, Inc., 99, 207
Saroyan, William, 69, 85, 89, 127, 128
Sartre, Jean-Paul, 42, 53, 88, 110, 144
Schechner, Richard, 82
Schneider, Alan, 37–38
Screen writing, compared with theatrical writing, 27, 125
Script format, 170–185
"Script-in-hand" reading, 160
Seagull, The (Chekhov), 71
Search for Signs of Intelligent Life in the Universe, The (Wagner), 38–39
Seneca, 8
Sentence structure in dialogue, 139–142
Shaffer, Peter, 52, 94
Shakespeare, William, 19, 22, 24, 28, 42, 45, 52, 58, 78, 81, 89, 97, 100, 101, 105, 106, 107, 108, 116, 118, 127, 129, 141, 142
Shaw, George Bernard, 6, 29, 41, 122, 136, 149, 160
Shepard, Sam, 17, 18, 32, 41, 78, 89, 105, 128
Shock of Recognition, The (Anderson), 101–106
"Show" versus "tell," 6, 19–21, 57–58, 61, 99
Simenon, Georges, 48
Simon, Danny, 52, 74
Simon, Neil, 32, 46, 52, 73, 74, 150, 153
Sister Mary Ignatius Explains It All for You (Durang), 53, 157
Six elements of drama (Aristotle), 123
Society of Authors' Representatives (SAR), 196
Soldier's Play, A (Fuller), 44, 52
Soliloquy, 40, 123, 145
Sophocles, 69
Speech writing, compared to theatrical writing, 125

Stage directions, 68, 148, 174–175
Stanislavski, Konstantin, 58, 91
Steinem, Gloria, 49
Strange Interlude (O'Neill), 44
Streetcar Named Desire, A (Williams), 27, 52, 83, 84, 97, 106–107, 127, 130, 143, 148
Strindberg, August, 1, 65
Summer and Smoke (Williams), 202
Swimming to Cambodia (Gray), 39, 204
Synge, John Millington, 41

Talking With . . . (Martin), 38
Talley's Folly (Wilson), 204
Television, influences of, xvi, 27
Ten-minute play, 41–42
Theater (journal), 199
Theatre Communications Group, 188–189
Theatre Profiles (Theatre Communications Group), 189
Theme: amplifying, 57–58; and dialogue, 127; starting a play with, 50, 53
Time, unity of, 30–33, 36
Timebends (Miller), 14
Time of Your Life, The (Saroyan), 85, 89, 128
Torch Song Trilogy (Fierstein), 53
Tru (Allen), 38
Twirler (Martin), 135
Two-character plays, 42–43

Unities of time, place, action, 30–33; in one-acts, 42–43
Updike, John, 16

Van Druten, John, 122, 130–131, 152

Wagner, Jane, 38
Waiting for Godot (Beckett), 30, 69, 78, 105, 118, 150, 191
Wait Until Dark (Knott), 51

Wake of Jamey Foster, The (Henley), 127, 130

Weiss, Peter, 23, 84

Wesker, Arnold, 13, 35

Where Are You Going, Hollis Jay? (Bradford), 67

Whiting, Frank, 2

Whoopi Goldberg (Goldberg), 39

Who's Afraid of Virginia Woolf? (Albee), 27, 69, 115, 126

Wilde, Oscar, 69, 115, 128

Wilder, Thornton, xiii, 11, 96, 99, 127

Williams, Tennessee, 13, 27, 49, 52, 83, 84, 87, 97, 99, 105, 106–107, 112–114, 127, 130, 138, 140–141, 142, 143, 144, 146, 148, 153–154, 202

Wilson, Lanford, 40, 41, 58–59, 64, 69, 71, 85–86, 87, 89, 145, 204

Workshop productions, 160–161

Workshops for playwrights, 200–202

Writer, The (magazine), 185, 199, 202

Writer's Digest (magazine), 185, 199, 202

Writer's Market (Writer's Digest Books), 198, 207

Writer's notebook, 54–55, 62–63. *See also* Journal, playwright's

Young, Stark, 104, 117

Zoo Story, The (Albee), 40, 43, 144–145, 148

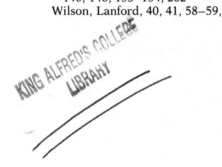